PRAYING
THE
PSALMS

EXPERIENCING
SCRIPTURE-FED
SPIRIT-LED
WORSHIP-BASED PRAYER

Volume 1 Psalms 1– 41

Daniel Henderson
General Editor

6:4PRESS
Praying the Psalms: Experiencing Scripture-Fed, Spirit-Led, Worship-Based Prayer
Volume 1 (1 - 41)
© Copyright 2021 by Strategic Renewal
Requests for information should be addressed to:
6:4PRESS, PO Box 370233, Denver, CO 80237
ISBN 978-1-7341973-3-4 softcover
To learn more about 6:4PRESS publishing opportunities
Contact: info@strategicrenewal.com

TABLE OF CONTENTS

PREFACE

For almost two decades I met with a small group of faithful church members every Sunday morning, typically at 6:30 a.m. Each week we would read a Psalm at the outset of our gathering. We would reflect on the truths we observed about God and His character. Then uniting prayers of praise and spontaneous song, we would spend the next 20 minutes worshiping from the word of God.

After a few moments of quiet surrender to the will and kingdom concerns of our Father, we would disperse throughout the church campus, praying with heartfelt requests for the needs of the day. Some would prayer walk in the area of the children's ministry, others would intercede for the youth in their section of the campus. Some would remain in the auditorium, walking among the rows, praying for receptive hearts during the upcoming service. I would often pray in the area of the choir loft and, of course, the pulpit.

At a designated time, we would re-gather in the front of the worship center as these faithful intercessors gathered around the worship pastor and me, asking for the Lord's favor on our leadership of the services. I often noted that the two of us were no more important in that moment, just more desperate.

Over the years, we went through the Psalms five times, simply praying from the next Psalm each week. I can testify that I learned how to pray in those weekly gatherings. Those 60-minute prayer experiences each Sunday ministered to my soul and prepared me to preach in ways that I still cannot fully articulate. It seemed that each Psalm was perfectly timed for the needs of the day and fueled our prayers of faith for the work of the Lord.

We would interact with each Psalm through the lens of the model prayer commanded by Jesus in Matthew 6:9-13 and Luke 11:2-4. The beautiful convergence of the truths in each Psalm with the rhythm of prayer taught by Christ was fresh and instructive every Sunday.

This guide will invite you to also experience the power of praying the Psalms, just as we did over those many years. I pray you will fully maximize this resource personally, in your family, and even in your church or broader ministry endeavors. I believe it will show you fresh pathways of transforming prayer.

Dietrich Bonhoeffer stated that "The Psalter is the great school of prayer" and that "We learn from the prayer of the Psalms what we should pray." [1] So, enter in to this school of prayer. Learn to pray more biblically, more honestly, and more faithfully.

Not long ago, I posted this thought on social media: "The great privilege of prayer is to open your Bible to experience a conversation with the Author who lives in you to explain what He meant by what He said and then inspire your heart to apply that truth in an intimate engagement that will transform your life – and empower you as an agent of gospel transformation in the world."

The author of the Psalms, ultimately the Holy Spirit, awaits your pursuit of the Lord in prayer. He will illumine, guide, comfort, convict, and change you. I truly pray, your journey through the Psalms in prayer will do as much for you as it has done for me – and even more.

For His glory,

Daniel Henderson
Founder and President of Strategic Renewal
Global Director, *The 6:4 Fellowship*

---

1 Dietrich Bonhoeffer, Life Together: The Classic Exploration of Christian Community (New York: Harper & Row, 1954), 47

CONTRIBUTORS

Daniel Henderson
GENERAL EDITOR
President, **Strategic Renewal,** *Global Director,* **The 6:4 Fellowship**
(www.strategicrenewal.com) (www.64fellowship.com)
Psalms 10, 38, 39, 40, 41

Justin Jeppesen—*Director of Spiritual Formation and Adjunct Professor, University of Northwestern, St. Paul, MN (www.unwsp.edu)*
Introduction, Appendix B,
Psalms 1, 11, 12, 13

Dennis Henderson—*Pastor, Fusion Bible Church, Durant, OK (www.fusiondurant.com)*
Psalms 9, 35, 36, 37

Jon Hoekema—*Pastor, Horizon Community Church, Downers Grove, IL (www.Horizoncc.org)*
Psalms 6, 26, 27, 28

Mike Mitchener—*Pastor, Riverview Baptist Church, Ripplemead, VA (www.riverviewtoday.org)*
Psalms 5, 23, 24, 25

Mike Moran—*Pastor, Creekside Evangelical Free Church, Merced, CA (www.creeksidemerced.org)*
Psalms 4, 20, 21, 22

Jeremiah Porter—*Pastor, Christ's Community Church, Granite Falls, WA (www.cfccchurch.org)*
Psalms 4, 20, 21, 22

Sandy Robertson—*Pastor, New Covenant Fellowship, Titusville, FL (www.ncftitusville.org)*
Psalms 2, 14, 15, 16

S. Lindsay Taylor—*President, Strategic Renewal, Canada, (www. strategicrenewal.ca)*
Psalms 3, 17, 18, 19

Aaron Telecky—*Pastor, Maranatha Bible Church, Cedar Rapids, IA (www.maranathabible.org)*
Psalms 7, 29, 30, 31

INTRODUCTION

By Justin Jeppesen

Music is one of the most powerful mediums of communication. It resonates in our core, eliciting emotion and longing. It calls forth transcendent thoughts and sometimes it even generates movement that alters the trajectory of our lives. Also, music draws out memories.

Have you ever heard a song on the radio or on a playlist that suddenly brings to the surface a memory that you had forgotten? Songs are often attached to memories, and memories bring alive past experiences, both the bad and the good. Imagine if you could go back through your life and write a song for each defining moment – every heartache, every celebration, trial, battle, victory. God already has. *For you.* It's called the Book of Psalms.

Music was a vital component of ancient Hebrew worship. In fact, the Book of Psalms could rightly be considered the original Old Testament "hymnal." Chapters were written in poetic form and most often sung as a part of Israel's worship and celebration. And like much music written through the centuries, it is no wonder that God, the divine musician, has wonderfully woven themes of joy and remembrance into His songs too.

Each Psalm "song" evokes memories of God's gracious dealings with His people, the nation of Israel. All collectively tell how God worked for His glory and their good throughout the multitude of their generations. Today, it could be said, Psalms is the "soundtrack" of God's redemptive history.

Just as songs, when we hear them, draw us back to reflect again on significant events in our personal lives, so too God sang songs over His nation calling them to remember Him and His ways. Yet these songs or Psalms were not only written *to* ancient Israel, they were also divinely composed *for* us. God has arranged divinely inspired songs for every season of our lives. Each Psalm has a unique way of giving breath and language to our life of prayer with our Creator. In the same way song lyrics or melodies enable us to articulate the deepest emotions of our hearts or clarify or even simplify puzzling concepts, so too the Psalms engage us at deep levels, especially when drawing us into the broad vocal register of prayer.

It would not be an overstatement to say that Psalms is one of the most popular and beloved books of the Bible. It is the "go to" book for many seeking encouragement and renewal of perspective. It draws from a wealth of experiences that apply to every aspect of human life. But the Psalms are not laid out in a neat and tidy order. Rather they appear unpredictable and dynamic as they flow from one theme to the next. This sense of random order seems to be strangely intentional. Individual Psalms often depict the reality and the dynamic unpredictability of life. Just as life may flow from a joyous occasion one moment, then – even suddenly – into a sorrowful moment the next, the Psalms meet us with a sincere and honest relevancy no matter our circumstances. In reading and thinking about the Psalms many have found refuge and strength, encouragement in tough times and especially, abiding joy.

This reality includes you! Even now, as you read this introduction the Lord is inviting you to encounter Him as you prayerfully engage in His divine songbook. The God of the Psalms desires to sing over you wherever you are in your journey and to bring you into a place of deeper trust and intimacy with Him.

THE PATHWAY TO JOYFUL PRAYER

While the 150 songs that compose the Book of Psalms display a striking diversity of themes they also present a unified focus. The original Hebrew title for Psalms is *"Tehillim,"* which translates into "Songs of Joy," or even more concisely, "Praises."[1] This is true even though the Psalms of lament, expressing sorrow, outnumber Psalms of praise, accompanied by celebrations of joy. And their order, sequence, and emphasis present a curious, yet insightful surprise. More times lament is the theme of early Psalms (there are 16 in the first 41 chapters). But only 4 are found in the final 43 chapters. Inversely, Psalms of joy are few at the beginning (only 7 in the first 41 chapters). Yet 13 erupt near the end of the entire collection, traveling an increasing crescendo of praise.

The point is this: Lament, sorrow, difficulty are eventually eclipsed by praise, joy, and gratitude at the end. One cannot help but wonder if this order intentionally models our life of faith as traveling pilgrims in this foreign land journeying toward our heavenly home. It is clear that songs of lament and praise go hand in hand to sustain a Godward focus in our praying.

Even now, human sorrows here on earth forge a trajectory toward a heavenly joy that can invade present circumstances. Learning to pray the Psalms as God's *Songs of Joy* equips His people to lay hold of the stunning

---

1. *An Introduction to the Old Testament.* Longman III, Tremper and Dillard B. Raymond. Zondervan, Grand Rapids, MI. 2006.

truths, strengths, and the multitude of comforts He designed to be tangibly experienced in everyday lives.

PRAYING LIKE JESUS

Of all the Scriptures cited in the New Testament, Psalms tops the list. The Lord Jesus himself quotes this joy-filled book over 50 times, often during occasions of great personal turmoil. They were, for Him, the songs of God, reminding Him of His Father and of Home. As a poignant example, Jesus quotes from the Psalms at the time of His greatest suffering on the cross. And what empowered Jesus to endure the agony of Calvary? According to Hebrews 12:2, it was "the joy that was set before him." Jesus was "a man of sorrows and acquainted with grief" (Isaiah 53:3), and yet, we powerfully see lament and joy converge at the cross. No wonder Jesus uses the Psalms in His dying breaths to extol His firm reliance upon and ultimate trust in His Heavenly Father (Psalm 22:1; Psalm 31:5). Even for Jesus the Psalms gave voice to His conversations with His Father and the Scriptures have been recorded to give us His example to emulate.

It's been said that if we can learn to pray as Jesus prayed we will have the power to live as Jesus lived. The good news is that Jesus did not leave His disciples guessing when it came to understanding *how* He prayed. He gave them the very rhythm of prayer modeled by His life and His words, especially found in what is commonly referred to as "The Lord's Prayer" (Matthew 6:9-13 – also Luke 11:2-4). The kind of prayer that Jesus' life exemplified was Scripture-fed, Spirit-led, and Worship-based. To the degree that we pray Scripture will be to the degree that we pray like Jesus. While more about Jesus' rhythm of prayer that He commanded us to follow is expounded upon in the next section *(see How to use this Guide),* suffice it to say that the Psalms provide an invaluable entry point to begin praying the way Jesus prayed.

A PERSONAL STORY OF TRANSFORMATION

It was the book of Psalms that the Holy Spirit used to teach me how to pray like Jesus prayed by engaging the Scriptures. When I was first introduced to Strategic Renewal and the 6:4 Fellowship, my life of prayer was transformed as I re-learned how to pray after Jesus' own pattern. The first place I applied this new way of praying was with the Psalms. As I began to practice worship-based prayer in God's songbook it opened before me a whole new realm of conversation with my Creator. It was like I was beginning to participate in the conversation that God had already initiated with me. Rather than coming to the Lord with a list of needs or feeling puzzled about what I should say, I began coming to Him with fresh eyes of faith, beholding His beauty, and with eager ears to listen to His voice. It was as if the Holy Spirit, as the divine conductor, began leading me through the sheet music of the Psalms to pray according to the diverse, yet unified melody of joy. When I allowed the Spirit-inspired words in the Psalms to shape the way I prayed, I began conversing with Jesus like He may have with His heavenly Father.

Praying the Psalms has cultivated, for me, a deep intimacy with God, established authentic connection with others, and has further equipped me for fruitful service within the local church. No matter what circumstance I have been in the Lord has met me time and again by animating my soul with songs of lament *and* joyful praise.

I referenced earlier the inverse, yet complementary relationship that is found between songs of lament and songs of praise. In 2020 I experienced this dynamic in a powerful and deeply personal way. After battling cancer for several months, the Lord brought my grandmother to her heavenly home. During my final conversation with her I read Psalms 145 through 150. As I read I often felt compelled to pause, praying a particular passage over her again. As I neared the end I was profoundly struck with the repetition of a single phrase, "Praise the Lord!" In those last moments with my grandmother, lament and sadness were overcome with a supernatural joy and peace. I realized that her faint and final breaths were, nonetheless, exclamations of the strongest praise as she was preparing to meet her Savior face to face. The final moments of my grandma's life on earth were matching the crescendo of praise we find in Psalms 145-150.

Just days later I awoke early in the morning to find a message on my phone saying that she had departed for heaven. My knees hit the floor. The first words that passed through my lips were, I believe, the same words my grandmother was then saying at that very moment, "Praise the Lord!" The Lord used the Psalms not only to shape the last conversation I had with her, but also to further fuel a lasting joy and praise that sustains my soul.

BEGINNING YOUR JOURNEY

Taking the cue from the original purpose of Psalms as a book of promise and joyful remembrance for ancient Israel, it has been my desire in recent years to regularly read and pray through the Psalms for the rest of my life. It is my prayer that this guide, and those that follow, combined with the recording of your own personal prayer journey in the "Journal for Experiencing Scripture-fed, Spirit-led, Worship-based Prayer" will mobilize you and other members of the Body of Christ to engage in transforming conversations with God that will have life-long and multi-generational impact.

A CALL TO CORPORATE PRAYER
Pray alone or with others?

People often ask, "Which is more important, private prayer or corporate prayer?" Our answer is a resounding, "Yes!" This is like asking which leg do we need to walk, the right or the left. Sadly, in Western culture we have essentially amputated our corporate prayer leg and are often lame on our private prayer leg. A healthy and biblical balance in prayer requires diligence in both.

Theologian D.A. Carson affirmed this principle, "Many facets of Christian discipleship, not the least prayer, are more effectively passed on by modeling than from teaching. Good praying is more easily caught than taught. We should choose models from whom we can learn."[2]

As Albert Mohler has aptly noted about the model prayer commanded by Jesus,

> There is no first-person singular pronoun in the entire prayer… One of the besetting sins of evangelicalism is our obsession with individualism. This obsession with individualism chronically besets us as evangelicals. The first-person singular pronoun reigns in our thinking. We tend to think about nearly everything (including the truths of God's Word) only as they relate to me. This is why when Jesus teaches his disciples to pray, He emphasizes from the very outset that we are part of a corporate people called the church.[3]

We learn best to pray by breaking the chains of rugged individualism and consistently gathering with others to learn to pray, to grow more effective in prayer, and to enjoy the richness of a fellowship only experienced together in prayer – especially Scripture-fed, Spirit-led, worship-based prayer.

While we know this experience of praying the Psalms will enrich your personal prayer life we also encourage you to join others on a very regular basis to practice this biblical approach to prayer. Of course, we trust this tool will be helpful in your marriage, family, and close friendships. If you do not already participate in a group at your church – start one, utilizing this resource. In this way, you can play an essential role in helping your faith community become "a house of prayer for all nations."

---

2. D. A. Carson, *A Call to Spiritual Reformation* (Grand Rapids: Baker, 1992), 35.
3. Albert Mohler *from https://albertmohler.com/2018/08/20/danger-christian-prayer/.*

HOW TO USE THIS PRAYER GUIDE

Prayer begins in Scripture. For it is in the Bible that our Lord shows His disciples how to pray. In Matthew 6:9-13 – often known as "the Lord's Prayer" – Jesus provides a pattern for prayer and commands that His disciples "pray in this way" (v. 9).

There are four "movements" that compose this divine symphony modeled in Christ's prayer. *Reverence. Response. Requests. Readiness.* Praying through each of these sequentially follows the pattern Christ Himself established. In obedience, when we pray in this way, we are praying God's way. Note the intent of each of the four movements:

"Our Father in Heaven, hallowed be your name." *Reverence (Upward)* begins with acknowledging the wonder, majesty, and character of God. With an open Bible in front of us, we ask: "Who are you Lord God? What have you revealed about Yourself in this section of Scripture? How do I honor You?"

"Your Kingdom come, Your will be done on earth as it is in heaven." *Response (Downward)* arises from the worshiping human heart. All I am surrendering to the revelation of all He is. In this movement we yield our will to His, our mind and agenda to Him. Often this response can be guided by the passage in front of us and by asking, "Given what these verses say about You, How do You want me to respond to You today, Father?"

"Give us this day our daily bread and forgive us our debts as we also have forgiven our debtors." *Requests (Inward)* emerge as the simple answers to the question, "What should I pray about?" Allow the verses you are considering in the moment to guide your *requests* in connection to both resources and relationships.

 **"And lead us not into temptation, but deliver us from evil (or 'the evil one')."** This is a cry for *Readiness, (Outward)* to be made ready for spiritual battle. What will we face today in a sinful and hostile world? Strong encouragement can be gleaned from the text we have been considering in this moment of prayer. That is why "praying the Scriptures" is so vital, and why Jesus commanded we follow this pattern. It is God's way to best overcome the attacks of the enemy. And in this way we are energized all the more when reading – or memorizing even – God's Word (Matthew 4:1-10; Ephesians 6:17).

When we "pray in this way" we are following Jesus' clear pattern for His disciples. That is why "the Lord's Prayer" remains a model and pattern for all future prayer, pray-ers, and praying.

Did those disciples, in the early chapters of Matthew understand what Jesus was getting at with this prayer pattern? Did they employ this model in their subsequent prayers? It seems so. Found in Acts 4:24-31 is the first recorded prayer of the disciples. It occurs upon the release of Peter and John from trial and confinement by the religious leaders of their day. This is how they prayed:

> *And when they heard it, they lifted their voices together to God and said, "Sovereign Lord, who made the heaven and the earth and the sea and everything in them,*
> **– REVERENCE**

> *who through the mouth of our father David, your servant, said by the Holy Spirit, 'Why did the Gentiles rage, and the peoples plot in vain? The kings of the earth set themselves, and the rulers were gathered together, against the Lord and against his*

Anointed'— for truly in this city there were gathered together against your holy servant Jesus, whom you anointed, both Herod and Pontius Pilate, along with the Gentiles and the peoples of Israel, to do whatever your hand and your plan had predestined to take place.
– RESPONSE

And now, Lord, look upon their threats and grant to your servants to continue to speak your word with all boldness while you stretch out your hand to heal, and signs and wonders are performed through the name of your holy servant Jesus."
– REQUESTS

And when they had prayed, the place in which they were gathered together was shaken, and they were all filled with the Holy Spirit and continued to speak the word of God with boldness.
– READINESS

In this first volume of **Praying the Psalms** (Psalms 1-41) we invite you to experience *Scripture-Fed, Spirit-Led, Worship-based Prayer*. It is designed to guide you through each of the four model prayer movements, using the individual Psalms to provoke your prayers.

The Psalms are individually set apart for you to encounter God personally and speak with Him. Supplemental commentary by 6:4 Fellowship pastors is provided for additional insight. The variety of approaches and interactions with each Psalm reflects the variety of gifts, viewpoints, and experiences of the contributors, which itself mirrors the multi-faceted Body of Christ. You may choose to meditate on and pray through a single Psalm for several days using the multiple prayer prompts provided.

There are two pages set aside for you to interact with each Psalm – a "left-hand page" and a "right-hand page." The following is a suggested method for **Praying the Psalms**. We invite you to "pray in this way."

- Select a Psalm you wish to pray through (in any order you may choose). Read it from your preferred translation or version of the Bible. (Perhaps, read it more than once.)

- Read the brief comments section found on the "left-hand page." There is room in the margins of that page for any personal notes you might wish to record.

- On the "right-hand page," under the
  <u>*Reverence*</u> *(Upward)* heading you will see several thoughts about God that are in that particular Psalm, His character, His attributes, His
  Holy Person. Ponder those. Celebrate Him.

- Next, you will see various suggestions ("prompts") for how you
  might declare back to the Lord the characteristics this particular Psalm has revealed about Him. Pick one or two and rejoice
  in Him, for He is worthy of our praise.

- Similarly, as you move down that page and
  come to the <u>*Response*</u> *(Downward)* section, there
  are several prompts that may stimulate your
  soul's reflection. Pick one or two and thank
  God for Who He is and how He has delighted
  your heart.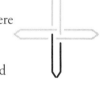

- As you arrive at the <u>*Requests*</u> *(Inward)* portion
  of your prayer time, remember He already
  knows your needs. (He knows how many
  hairs you have on your head! – Matthew
  10:30, Luke 12:7). Here use one or two of
  the suggested prompts to align your heart with His purposes,
  asking Him for His help and His outcomes in your life.

- <u>*Readiness,*</u> *(Outward)* is the final movement of
  prayer. Spiritual war is real and prayer is our
  most effective weapon against the diversions,
  distractions, and divisions of the adversary
  (2 Corinthians 10:3-5, Ephesians 6:18). Pray
  through one or two of the prompts inviting
  God's mercy and protection for yourself and His empowering
  for resistance against the enemy in the battle for our lives.

We trust you will enjoy and appreciate **Praying the Psalms** as you encounter our wonderful Lord. It is our prayer that you flourish in a lifetime
of praying God's way, following the example of Jesus, serving others in and
by the Holy Spirit, and glorifying the Father (Matthew 5:14-16). Blessings
to you in the journey and in the delight of prayer that awaits you.

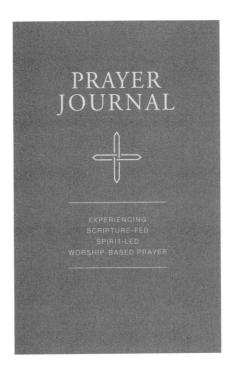

A separate and companion book,
Prayer Journal for Experiencing Scripture-Fed,
Spirit-Led, Worship-Based Prayer,
is also available. We encourage its use in
recording your ongoing encounters with God,
both as you are in the midst of prayer and as you
reflect back on how He has made Himself known to
you and answered your prayers.

(store.strategicrenewal.com)

PSALM 1

Comments by Justin Jeppesen
Author   Unknown
Category Wisdom
In Brief This Gateway to the Book of Psalms reveals two contrasting paths to life. They lead to two different outcomes. Only one can be chosen.

As a wisdom Psalm, this song lays the foundation for the entire Book of Psalms and contains a microcosm of the entirety of the Book's teaching. The author displays the kind of person who is wise and blessed and the kind of person who embodies wickedness. They are set alongside one another in stark contrast. Vivid imagery describes the divergent outcomes of the "way of the righteous" and the "way of the wicked."

Psalm 1 opens with a benediction, declaring and describing the one who is blessed. The blessed person does not succumb to the destructive progression of sin, which leads from bad to worse. Rather, the blessed finds delight in the word of God and thinks deeply about it ("meditates on it day and night"). Since the blessed one is rooted and nourished in the soil of God's word, the Lord Himself watches over him or her with intimate favor and protection. The outcome of this chosen path is described as a life that is "planted," "fruitful," and "prosperous" no matter what the circumstances may be.

Conversely, the ways of the wicked are rootless, wind tossed, and have no footing or place of welcome among God's covenant people. This path will not prosper them, but instead it leads to judgment and death.

Psalm 1 anticipates Jesus' Sermon on the Mount (Matthew 5-7), which also begins with a benediction describing the blessed person in His kingdom and ends with two contrasting scenarios of those who wisely obey Christ's word or foolishly disobey. Will you build your house upon the solid unchanging rock or upon the shifting sands of current culture or emotion?

Will you choose the path of the righteous or succumb to the way of the wicked? There is no greater way to delight in and meditate upon the law of the Lord than to pray through it. Prayer unlocks the wisdom of obedience and guards against the foolishness of disobedience. Praying this and other Psalms grows deep roots in the soil of God's sustaining word. Praying over God's word "day and night" cultivates our appetite for the ways of God.

Just as the people of ancient Israel prayerfully sang this song of wisdom to remind them of the foundation of their lives and their final destiny, so we too can pray it in our day, reminding ourselves that Jesus is our cornerstone and pathway to abundant life.

PSALM 1 – GUIDE

REVERENCE – *Identify and celebrate God's praiseworthy attributes*

- He is a God of blessing; the source of truth and delight – vv. 1-2
- He is our sustainer and the source of our fruitfulness – v. 3
- He is the all knowing Judge of the wicked and the righteous – vv. 4-6

Prayer Prompts
- Thank You that You have been my source of blessing in …
- I delight in Your Law because …
- Like a tree firmly planted by water You have given me …

RESPONSE – *Surrender to Him and His ways*

- I confess I have sat, walked, and stood in the paths of the ungodly when …
- I surrender my heart afresh that I may meditate more faithfully on Your truth.

REQUESTS – *Ask the Spirit to guide your prayer over concerns, resources, and relationships*

- Help me to delight in Your Law when I am tempted to …
- I am trusting You to sustain me and allow me to bear fruit as I…
- Give me an urgency to graciously share Your truth with the "wicked" when I …

READINESS – *Encouragement and strength for spiritual battle*

- When I am prone to doubt, remind me that You know my way when …

PSALM 2

Comments by Sandy Robertson
Author   David
Category   Royal/Prophetic
In Brief   Describes the foolishness of any nation that rebels against
               the supreme authority of God and His Son.

A wise pastor once said, "If you are going to preach from the Old Testament, you better get to Jesus in a hurry." Psalm 2 gets to Jesus in a hurry. You can't miss the prophetic references to the Son of God in the Psalm (v. 2 "His Anointed"; v. 6 "My King"; v. 7 "My Son … I have begotten You"; v. 12 "Kiss the Son … Trust in Him"). In the New Testament, the apostles quote Psalm 2 directly (Acts 4:25-26; Acts 13:33) regarding the divine purposes of God in sending His Son into the world and allowing him to be crucified by the religious and political rulers of his day.

The Son of God appears in the Psalms as either a Suffering Savior (i.e. Ps. 22) or, as here, a Triumphant King. Psalm 2 celebrates the victory of God's chosen King and His ultimate rule over all nations. He is the coming King who will establish His reign "on earth as it is in heaven."

The Psalm falls naturally into four parts …

1. The Nations Raging (vv. 1-3) … the folly of fighting against God.
2. The Lord Laughing (vv. 4-6) … the fate of the enemies to God.
3. The Lord Declaring (vv. 7-9) … the favor upon the Son of God.
4. The Nations Choosing (vv. 10-12) … the forewarning and judgment of God.

Psalm One begins with the word "Blessed" and teaches us what a blessed man looks like. Psalm Two ends with the word "Blessed" and teaches us what a blessed nation looks like. It will be populated by people "whose God is the Lord." (cf. Ps. 33:12)

"A fool has said in his heart there is no God" (Ps. 14:1). Likewise, it is a foolish nation whose leaders and people say, "We will not have this Man to reign over us" (Luke 19:14).

PSALM 2 – GUIDE

REVERENCE – *Identify and celebrate God's praiseworthy attributes*

- Christ is Lord and the Anointed One – v. 2
- He sits enthroned in the Heavens; Jesus is King; He is Holy – vv. 4-6
- The nations of the earth belong to Him – v. 8
- Christ will judge and rule the nations – v. 9
- He is Worthy of our service, reverence, fand affection – vv. 11-12
- He is both Judge and the source of blessing and refuge – v. 12

Prayer Prompts

- I praise You Jesus because You are King over …
- Because the whole earth is Your possession, You are Lord over …
- Thank You that You were my refuge when …

RESPONSE – *Surrender to Him and His ways*

- Holy King, I surrender my … to Your rule.

REQUESTS – *Ask the Spirit to guide your prayer over concerns, resources, and relationships*

- King Jesus, even though … I know that You will someday rule the nations.
- I know that … *(name)* is in rebellion against You. Use me to call them to serve and worship You.
- Help me to serve and worship You today as I …

READINESS – *Encouragement and strength for spiritual battle*

- As I encounter … help me to trust You as my refuge.

PSALM 3

Comments by S. Lindsay Taylor
Author   David
Category   Lament
In Brief   While he deals with the rebellion of his son Absalom,
               David is encouraged by God's protection.

Clearly linked to an historical event, Psalm 3 is one of 14 others connected to a major event in David's life. The detailed look at David fleeing his rebellious and vengeful son is recorded in 2 Samuel 15:13ff.

This Psalm has a simple outline with each point containing two verses:
1. Complaint (vv. 1-2) – He listens to the wrong voice and wonders, does God care?
2. Confidence (vv. 3-4) – He is refreshed in the knowledge of answered prayer.
3. Cover (vv. 5-6) – He sings of safety in the midst of danger.
4. Consolation (vv. 7-8) – He strengthens himself in the Lord.

David begins with a passionate expression of grief over his son's rebellion and disloyalty. Unfortunately, we all understand the pain of someone being disloyal. The experience of betrayal is always a test. Will we lose heart? Will we push on? David's enemies had even questioned his faith and his God. That being said, with a heart full of pain, mingled with confidence, David looks up (v. 3). He has absolute confidence in the ability of a sovereign God to provide and protect. His confidence rested in the very nature of God; He is a "shield about me," David says. God's imminent protection is just one of the many praiseworthy attributes we see in this Psalm that can cause our hearts to rejoice as we look up to Him!

Despite David's weary heart, he worships God. Immediately his focus is transferred from his detractors to his glorious redeemer (v. 4). Rather than relying on himself, David finds consolation and life-giving refreshment in God (v. 5). David's request in verse 7 is urgent and compelling. "Arise, Oh Lord, Save me, Oh my God." David's confidence is so strong that he is certain his enemies would run away. Why? Because victory is a done deal! We may have this same confidence as we navigate life. As the Apostle Paul reminds believers in Romans, "We are more than conquerors." It is enough for the Lord to "stand up," and all will be well. The Psalm concludes with a glorious, triumphant note of praise (v. 8). Let us praise Him, as victory in my life and yours belongs to the Lord.

PSALM 3 – GUIDE

REVERENCE – *Identify and celebrate God's praiseworthy attributes*

- Our God is in the midst of difficulties – v. 1
- He is a shield/protector during trouble – v. 3
- We glory in Him who lifts our head/gives us hope – v. 3
- He is Holy and He hears and answers our cries for help – v. 4
- Sustains us and gives us rest – v. 5
- Dispels our fears and saves/delivers us from our enemies – vv. 6-7
- God of salvation and source of blessing for His people – vv. 8-9

Prayer Prompts

- Even though I am facing … *(opposition)* I know You are my shield.
- Thank You that You lifted my head and gave me hope when …
- Thank You that You have blessed me already with …

RESPONSE – *Surrender to Him and His ways*

- I confess that I have listened to doubts and accusations about …
- I surrender these and look to You alone.
- I surrender my fears about … trusting You to deliver me.

REQUESTS – *Ask the Spirit to guide your prayer over concerns, resources, and relationships*

- I trust You to be my shield today as I encounter …
- Because You are my sustainer, I will not be afraid of …
- Help … *(name)* to glory in You today, finding hope and deliverance in You.
- Because You are a God who blesses Your people, I am asking You to bless … *(name)*.

READINESS – *Encouragement and strength for spiritual battle*

- "Today, I trust You to save me from the enemies of …"

Salvation belongs to you!

PSALM 4

Comments by Mike Moran
Author David
Category Lament
In Brief Based on his knowledge of God and according to His character, David cries out for help against his enemies, who oppose him at every turn.

David faces seemingly non-stop opposition from those who sought his destruction. Some came from those within his own household (Absalom, his son) along with some from within the community. As is his practice, when facing all kinds of challenges, David cries out to God for help. David's long and intimate personal relationship with God and his understanding of His Creator's character form the basis of his requests. David appeals to God because he knows God answers prayer. He asks God for mercy because he knows God is merciful. He asks God for relief because he knows and has experienced this relief on other occasions during his life. David then goes on to speak to his opponents. He expresses bewilderment with their continual resistance to God's truth. He then assures them that God will hear his cry and answer his prayer. David directs his enemies to, therefore, repent, to begin to live differently in three ways:

1) Do not let your anger lead you to sin
2) Quietly reflect upon the condition of your heart
3) Start offering right sacrifices to God

David addresses what many were asking, "Who can show us any good?" He immediately provides an answer, asking God to take action. "Let the light of your face shine upon us, O LORD." For David had experienced the light of the LORD'S face throughout his life journey. He knew God desired people to know Him and that experiencing His light would provide answers to their questions.

David concludes with a moment of praise. God has "filled my heart with greater joy" and "I will lie down and sleep in peace, for you alone, O LORD, make me dwell in safety." Like David, take a few minutes to recount the ways you have experienced the Lord's "shining face," both in facing opposition and in experiencing a heart-filled joy that has enabled you to "sleep in peace and safety."

PSALM 4 – GUIDE

REVERENCE – *Identify and celebrate God's praiseworthy attributes*

- Hears our prayers and answers when we call in our distress – v. 1
- Gracious and Righteous and the source of our righteousness – v. 1
- Good, trustworthy and worthy of our sacrifices – vv. 5-6
- Is the source of surpassing joy, peace and safety – vv. 7-8

Prayer Prompts
- I praise You that You heard my prayer when …
- I praise You that You are righteous, and make me righteous, even though …
- I praise You that You provided relief in my distress when …

RESPONSE – *Surrender to Him and His ways*

- When the world seeks to … set my heart apart to You alone.
- When I struggle with anger over … let me trust You in a spirit of quiet surrender.

REQUESTS – *Ask the Spirit to guide your prayer over concerns, resources, and relationships*

- Lord, I give myself to You and trust You today for …
- Even though the world doubts You, let me see and seek Your goodness in …
- I trust You for Your surpassing joy today, even though …

READINESS – *Encouragement and strength for spiritual battle*

- Even though I continue to encounter … *(spiritual battles)* give me Your peace.

PSALM 5

Comments by Mike Mitchener

Author   David

Category Lament

In Brief God uses David's adversaries to chasten him, yet he trusts in God's deliverance.

Psalm 5 is a morning Psalm designed by God to get our hearts and souls prepared for the day ahead. It seems as if the world around us is becoming altogether unscrupulous. Many in today's culture feel free to put their godlessness on display. And it causes us to groan. Psalm 5 is a reminder that humanity is no more corrupt today than he has always been. King David looked around and groaned about the wicked, rebellious evildoers, the boastful liars, the bloodthirsty, deceitful men, and the false flatterers with no truth in their mouths. They seemingly surrounded him.

Perhaps he was exhausted and discouraged from fighting the wicked for the soul of his nation the previous day, and he saw no end in sight. So, early in the morning, King David took his lament over the condition of his nation to his King. King David reminds himself, "My God gets the final word." The Lord will judge the wicked. The Lord will reward the righteous. King David reminds the righteous that God is our refuge, our shelter and protection when we are in danger or distress. And we can rejoice in the midst of difficulty even calamity, knowing the Lord will bless the righteous and God's favor will cover us. So, the enemy may *seem to be* winning, but take refuge in Him. Rejoice knowing He is your shield. You do not have to be dismayed or discouraged, your hope is in Him!

> *Lord, I lift my voice to worship and exalt You early in the morning. It brings me joy knowing You are my refuge. Help me stay faithful to Your straight path as I walk in the midst of a crooked and perverse generation.*

Psalm 5 – Guide

REVERENCE – *Identify and celebrate God's praiseworthy attributes*

- God hears our prayer and considers our groanings/laments – v. 1
- He is God and King – v. 2
- Holy and pure, He meets us morning by morning – vv. 3-4
- He resists the proud and evil heart and judges lies and deception – vv. 5-6
- Is abundant in steadfast love – v. 7
- He leads and directs us and is righteous – v. 8
- Judges transgressors and rebels – vv. 9-10
- He is our refuge, our joy and our protection, worthy of exaltation – v. 11
- He blesses the righteous; He is our shield – v. 12

Prayer Prompts

- I praise You Lord that You heard my cry for help when …
- Because You are King, I know that You can …
- Thank You that I have experienced Your steadfast love when …
- Holy One, I bow down before You in fear because You are …

RESPONSE – *Surrender to Him and His ways*

- Lord, You know that right now my groanings and cries are the result of … I come in full surrender, giving these things to You.
- Because You do not delight in wickedness, I confess …

REQUESTS – *Ask the Spirit to guide your prayer over concerns, resources, and relationships*

- In the spiritual battle I face, I am trusting in You to lead me as I …
- I ask for Your joy as I trust in You to be my refuge when …
- Because … *(names)* love Your name, spread Your protection over them as they …

READINESS – *Encouragement and strength for spiritual battle*

- Lord, may Your favor be my shield today as I encounter… *(area of spiritual battle).*

PSALM 6

Comments by Jon Hoekema
Author   David
Category Lament
In Brief   David's cry for healing and deliverance when he was very ill, when his enemies were causing him added emotional pain, all the while trusting that God hears him.

This is a Psalm of confession and humility before God. It is the first of seven, (Psalms 6, 32, 38, 51, 102, 130, 143) *Penitential Psalms* where the writers cry out to God. Their sins have caused them physical and emotional anguish. All follow the theme of humility before God with the hope that He will restore them to health and to the joy of living in His grace.

In Psalm 6, David is exhausted from physical pain and emotional stress (vv. 2, 6). David attributes his sickness as God's punishment of his sin. While we don't often think about illness that way today, it was common throughout Scripture. For instance, in John 9:2, the disciples ask Jesus, "who sinned, this man or his parents, that he was born blind?"

David cries out, "How long, O Lord, how long?" (v. 3). Because David has a close relationship with God and understands Him, he is able to wrestle with God about his pains and disappointments. This is the beauty of Psalms of Lament. God invites us to cry out to Him in our pain, in our brokenness, in our sin, in our difficulties and to trust in His gracious sovereignty. Because of our relationship with Jesus Christ we implore God, as David did, to deliver us, not because we deserve it, but because of His unfailing love (v. 4).

In verse 6, David cries that he is worn out from groaning. This verse is the very center of the Psalm in the original Hebrew. It is an oft-used literary technique to point the reader to the main theme. And the Lord hears his cry for mercy. David doesn't see the reality of that hope coming to pass, but there *is* hope.

Sometimes in our lives, while we have significant pain, trouble, and hardships, the best we can offer one another and the best we can hold onto ourselves is hope. We can't explain away the pain. Religious platitudes don't work. They seldom make us feel better. Instead, acknowledge the reality that this is not the way it's supposed to be. And in that hold to the hope that God hears our cries for mercy and our prayers for help. He will not abandon us to the grave, but will ultimately show those who believe the light of life.

Psalm 6 – Guide

REVERENCE – *Identify and celebrate God's praiseworthy attributes*

- Rebukes and Disciplines – v. 1
- Gracious Healer – v. 2
- Deliverer and our steadfast love – v. 4
- Hears our weeping and accepts our prayers – vv. 8-9

Prayer Prompts
- Lord, I praise You that You have been gracious to me when …
- Thank You for hearing and answering me when I cried out to You about …

RESPONSE – *Surrender to Him and His ways*

- I surrender my trouble … I will patiently wait for Your response.
- Lord, I confess my weariness about … and trust that You will bring deliverance.
- I repent of my impatience and doubt as I wait for You to answer my cry for …

REQUESTS – *Ask the Spirit to guide your prayer over concerns, resources, and relationships*

- Lord, please bring Your deliverance to … *(name)* and help them look to You alone.
- For the sake of Your steadfast love, bring salvation to … *(name)*.
- Because You know my weeping about … please sustain me so I can give You praise!

READINESS – *Encouragement and strength for spiritual battle*

- O Lord, cause workers of evil to depart from my … *(battles, temptations)*
- Turn back and put to shame the enemies present in … *(person, circumstance)*

The Lord has heard my cry!

PSALM 7

Comments by Aaron Telecky
Author   David
Category   Lament
In Brief   A plea to God, the righteous judge, to protect His servant and do justice to His enemies.

Despite initially being shrouded in a bit of mystery (the meaning of Shiggaion is uncertain and Cush the Benjamite does not appear elsewhere in Scripture), what is clear is that David wrote this Psalm in what was, to him, an all-too-familiar place: on the run from dangerous, real-life enemies. To that end, he begins with an urgent cry for God's protection from imminent danger (vv. 1-2). Then, having apparently found room to breathe, he prayerfully explores his situation.

One possibility David acknowledges before God is that the trouble he's in could be his own fault and, if so, he is willing to come clean and face the natural consequences of his actions (vv. 3-5). Even so, David also understood that those pursuing him were nasty characters doing harm to the Lord's people. Through the remainder of the Psalm he alternately prays that God will deliver the justice to his enemies which they deserve. At the same time protecting His people and vindicating David specifically since he believes the attacks he was enduring were unwarranted.

Then in conclusion, having poured his heart out to the Lord in prayer, David finishes this Psalm in typically triumphant fashion (v. 17), giving thanks in prayer, in praise, and in song to God in anticipation of His faithful answers. And while the difficult circumstances we face in life will differ from those David faced here, his prayer is a model one for us. Oftentimes – perhaps far more often than we care to admit – the Lord doesn't immediately swoop in and answer our cries for help. However, when we pray to Him as openly, honestly, and biblically as David did, God will show up and change our hearts, enabling us to sing His praises even while the darkness lingers.

Psalm 7 – Guide

REVERENCE – *Identify and celebrate God's praiseworthy attributes*

- The Lord God is my refuge, savior and deliverer from spiritual enemies – vv. 1-3
- The One who knows my heart and judges the integrity of life – vv. 3-5, 8
- He is the judge of my spiritual enemies and rules all people – vv. 6-9
- The one who establishes the righteous, testing every mind and heart – v. 9
- The shield and savior of the upright; righteous Judge of all – vv. 10-16
- Lord Most High, worthy of praise for His name and righteousness sake – v. 17

Prayer Prompts

- Lord, my God, I praise You that You have been my refuge when . . .
- My righteous God, I praise You that You will ultimately judge . . .
- Lord Most High, I praise You because Your name is . . .

RESPONSE – *Surrender to Him and His ways*

- Because You know my mind and heart and judge my integrity, I confess . . . *(areas of disobedience, spiritual failure, relational struggle, etc.)*

REQUESTS – *Ask the Spirit to guide your prayer over concerns, resources, and relationships*

- Today I trust You to shield me and be my savior as I deal with . . .
- Because You establish the righteous, I pray that You will establish . . . in my life.
- Because You establish the righteous, I pray for . . . *(name)* that You will . . .

READINESS – *Encouragement and strength for spiritual battle*

- Lord, as I enter a world filled with spiritual opposition, I will trust You will deliver me from enemies of . . .

PSALM 8

Comments by Jeremiah Porter
Author   David
Category   Praise
In Brief   A celebration of the majesty of God and the dignity of
               humanity.

A proper understanding of who we are begins with understanding who God is and how we relate to Him. God is LORD, the one true and only God, and our Lord, our master and ruler. His name - His revealed nature and character - is full of distinguished greatness over all of creation (v. 1). He is so majestic that even children and infants can recognize Him and give Him praise. His evident character silences the wicked notion that there is no God (v. 2). God is the creator of the universe filled with stars and the moon, which He placed with His own fingers (v. 3). God is incomparably awesome; He is so big and powerful that in observing the created order, His glory and majesty are visible from anywhere on earth.

So then, in light of who God is, what are we? As Creator and Sustainer of all, does He even notice us or care about us (v. 4)? The clear answer is, "Yes!" Of all creation, God made humans in His image and crowned them with the glorious dual purpose of both knowing Him and representing Him as they rule over His creation (vv. 5-8). This profound responsibility loudly affirms the value of humanity to God. The author of Hebrews quotes Psalm 8:5-7 as a prophetic word about who Jesus is and what He has done to restore us to God (Heb. 2:9), enabling us to once again do a good work with and for God - a life full of dignity, honor, and worth. So valuable are we to Him that even our sin did not diminish us in God's eyes.

As we pray Psalm 8, we can praise God for His majestic nature and character revealed to us in creation and in His word. We can praise God for how we have experienced His awesome power and glory in our own lives. We can surrender ourselves to the reality of our utter dependence upon God in order to have life, new life in Christ, and a life full of glory and honor. Finally, we can seek Him for wisdom and strength to do the work He has called us to do in a way that represents Him well.

PSALM 8 – GUIDE

REVERENCE – *Identify and celebrate God's praiseworthy attributes*

- His name is majestic, glorious in heaven and earth – vv. 1, 9
- His strength is displayed in and through the weak/vulnerable – v. 2
- He overpowers his enemies – v. 2
- His works are displayed in the heavens and He sets the world in place – v. 3
- He cares for us; He establishes our value and our role in His creation – vv. 4-8

Prayer Prompts

- I praise Your majesty because Your name is …
- Thank You that You display Your strength in and through us even when …
- I praise You that Your power is greater than …
- I thank You that I saw Your glory in the heavens when …
- Thank You that You have established our value, even when the world tries to tell us …

RESPONSE – *Surrender to Him and His ways*

- I acknowledge Your power and sovereignty in … I surrender my disordered heart/life.
- You set the worlds in place, so I trust You to bring order and stability to …
- Thank You that You are mindful of me and care for me when …

REQUESTS – *Ask the Spirit to guide your prayer over concerns, resources, and relationships*

- I pray that the majesty of Your name will be evident in my life today as I …
- I ask for Your strength today as I encounter the enemy of …
- I pray for … *(names)*, bring order and meaning to their lives as they struggle with …
- You have given me dignity and authority; help me be a faithful steward today as I …

READINESS – *Encouragement and strength for spiritual battle*

- Lord, fix my mind on Your majestic name and authority as I battle with …

Psalm 9

Comments by Dennis Henderson
Author David
Category Thanksgiving
In Brief David gives thanks for God's blessings in protecting him from his enemies.

As a "man after God's own heart" (Acts 13:22), David unreservedly gives his whole-hearted praise to God for all His wonderful deeds (v. 1). God has upheld his cause and has given "righteous judgment" (v. 4). The Jewish scholars believe this psalm is a reflection on the defeat of Goliath. God protected David from an overwhelming enemy. But God's power and protection was not limited to just Goliath. David recounts that God has rebuked nations, uprooted cities, and blotted out the wicked.

There is a blend of the infinite greatness and wonderful gentleness of God. He "sits enthroned forever" (v. 7) and "judges the world with righteousness" (v. 8). God is supreme in glory and might, yet, He is not far away and uncaring. Instead, He is a "stronghold for the oppressed, a stronghold in times of trouble" (v. 9). For this reason, "the needy shall not always be forgotten" (v. 18).

In Jesus Christ, we see these marks of God in beautiful flesh-and-blood reality. For Christ is both a lion and lamb (Rev. 5:5-6). He is both supremely powerful (2 Thess. 1:7-10) and supremely gentle (Matt. 11:28-29) as He invites the weary to come to Him for rest. Jesus is our strong refuge and a tender friend. In Jesus, we see concretely the God of Psalm 9 (vv. 9, 18, cf. Luke 4:18).

Let us join with David in our own great praise. When there is trouble, pray to God about it. What matters is that God still rules the world. So, praise God today. He is in control no matter how dark the season might seem. God still reigns and we trust Him for each day that He gives us.

Psalm 9 – Guide

REVERENCE – *Identify and celebrate God's praiseworthy attributes*

- He is worthy of wholehearted thanksgiving for His wonderful deeds – vv. 1, 11
- He is God Most High and worthy of glad exultation and songs of praise – vv. 2, 11
- He confounds our enemies and executes righteous judgment – vv. 3-4, 7-8
- He rebukes and ends the wicked – vv. 5-6, 15-17, 19-20
- He is our stronghold in times of trouble – v. 9
- He is trustworthy and desires to be known; He will not forsake seekers – v. 10
- His is enthroned before His people, remembering the cry of the afflicted and needy – vv. 12-13, 18
- He is gracious when we call on Him, He lifts us up from death – v. 12
- He gives us joy in His salvation, He is the hope of the poor – vv. 14, 18

Prayer Prompts

- Lord, with my whole heart, I want to thank You for …
- As I think of Your wonderful deeds in my life, I praise You for when You …
- I sing praise to You because Your name is …
- God Most High, You are exalted over …
- Thank You that when … *(times of personal trouble)*. You were my stronghold.

RESPONSE – *Surrender to Him and His ways*

- Because You are the righteous judge, I submit my unrighteous thoughts, words and deeds before You in humble confession. Specifically, I surrender …

REQUESTS – *Ask the Spirit to guide your prayer over concerns, resources, and relationships*

- Because Your name is … I will trust You for …
- I cry out to You for grace because … *(some area of affliction)*
- Be a stronghold for … *(name)* as they encounter the trouble of …
- Help me to tell of Your deeds/recount Your praises today as I …

READINESS – *Encouragement and strength for spiritual battle*

- Arise, O Lord, and help me to prevail over … *(area of temptation or evil)*

  I rejoice in Your salvation!

PSALM 10

Comments by Daniel Henderson
Author   Unknown
Category Lament
In Brief God seems far off while the wicked prey on the unfortunate.

Sometimes prayer is simply the raw outpouring of the soul haunted by doubts, overcome with fears, and even plagued with troubling questions. Psalm 10 begins with the question, "Why?" Our God is sovereign and He knows that we are not. He can handle our questions and agonizing confusion. Very often we cry out to God with a very limited perspective, yet with emotions that are very real in the moment.

Such is the case in Psalm 10. As we are often in our day, the Psalmist is overwhelmed and perplexed by the boastings and behaviors of the wicked, seemingly unchecked by divine justice. He feels surrounded by people who are blatantly godless and who prey on the helpless. It seems in the moment that God is not acting in bringing these evildoers to justice as they taunt God and torment the less fortunate. These scenes and perplexities seem all too real to us as we also watch with consternation.

When the writer eventually takes his eyes off the presenting situation and turns to God with an earnest cry (v. 12) he experiences the powerful reality of restored perspective. The truth of God's sovereignty, justice, and help for the helpless becomes clear. In fact, as prayer often does for all of us, the Psalmist's heart turns from despondency to a declaration of praise (vv. 16-18). He closes his prayer in confidence that the Lord is "King forever and ever" (v. 16). Our God hears our cries, strengthens our hearts, executes ultimate justice for the fatherless and oppressed. He will, in His final judgment, bring an end to the temporary parading of the wicked (vv. 17-18).

As you pray from Psalm 10, pour out your questions and consternations. Then, call on God to "arise" (v. 12) and act on behalf of His people. Claim the truths of vv. 14-18 and experience, once again, the power of prayer to transform your perspective as you see all things in light of the character and mighty deeds of the Lord.

PSALM 10 – GUIDE

REVERENCE – *Identify and celebrate God's praiseworthy attributes*
- God receives and responds to our questions and perplexities – vv. 1-11, 13
- He is a God of judgment – vv. 5, 12, 14-16, 18
- He sees all and remembers /hears our afflictions – vv. 12, 14, 17
- Cares for the helpless and the fatherless – v. 14
- King, Eternal, He hears us and strengthens our hearts – vv. 16-17
- Brings justice for his people – v. 18

Prayer Prompts
- I praise You Lord that when I questioned … You listened and responded
- I can trust You as King to judge the evil of this world, especially …
- I thank You for the assurance I have in knowing that You see …
- I praise You that You were my helper when …

RESPONSE – *Surrender to Him and His ways*
- Lord, today I ask "why" as I ponder … I surrender my questions to You and trust.
- I am in turmoil over … I submit my heart to You and will trust You to do justice.

REQUESTS – *Ask the Spirit to guide your prayer over concerns, resources, and relationships*
- Lord, I ask You to "arise" on behalf of … *(name)* and assure them of Your care.
- Lord, today I am feeling helpless over … and commit myself anew to You.
- As Helper to the fatherless, I pray that You care especially for … *(name)*.
- Lord, please strengthen the hearts of our church leaders by giving them …

READINESS – *Encouragement and strength for spiritual battle*
- Lord, even when we are helpless, we know You will confront the wickedness of …
- We trust You to judge … *(areas of wickedness)* in the nations of the world.

You are King forever and ever

PSALM 11

Comments by Justin Jeppesen
Author   David
Category   Confidence
In Brief   The Lord is the only trustworthy refuge, who, in His holiness, lovingly tests and delivers the righteous, while simultaneously bringing the wicked to sudden and final judgment.

This song focuses praise upon the Lord as our righteous refuge in times of trouble. As an individual song of confident praise, David draws upon his experiential knowledge of God's faithful protection in a time of crisis. This song was likely penned while David was on the run from King Saul who was seeking after his life (1 Samuel 19-23).

While on the run, David had decisions to make. To whom would he run, where would he seek safety? He must "flee like a bird" towards a mountain, for the wicked have the upright in heart "in their sights" and are ready to strike. Nevertheless, while an earthly king driven by wicked self-ambition was pursuing David, there was a heavenly King in residence Whose character is holy and Whose foundation is righteous. David's security in the face of dangerous and violent enemies is none other than the Lord himself.

This Lord is the King who sees and tests all. The Lord's loving holiness will test the righteous, cultivating deeper trust within His people. Conversely, He is vehemently opposed to the wicked, bringing them to sudden and final ruin.

The Psalm ends as it began, by confidently extolling the righteousness of God, both His character and His deeds. In the end, it is the upright who have the privilege of beholding the Lord's face and standing in His protective and Holy presence.

PSALM 11 – GUIDE

REVERENCE – *Identify and celebrate God's praiseworthy attributes*

- He is Jehovah, our personal, covenant-keeping God, our refuge – vv. 1-2
- He is righteous and the source of our righteousness – vv. 2-3, 5, 7
- He is Holy, all seeing, and enthroned in heaven – v. 4
- He tests the hearts of all and judges wickedness – vv. 4-6
- He loves righteousness and reveals Himself in intimacy to the upright – v. 7

Prayer Prompts

- I praise You, my Jehovah, especially in a world that is …
- You have empowered me to live righteously in my walk with You when …
- You are Holy because You are …
- I praise You that when I behold Your face, I see …

RESPONSE – *Surrender to Him and His ways*

- All-seeing, all-knowing Lord, as You test my heart right now, I confess …
- I confess that I am often troubled by the foundations being destroyed as I observe …
- Help me to keep my eyes on Your high and holy throne.

REQUESTS – *Ask the Spirit to guide your prayer over concerns, resources, and relationships*

- Help me trust You as my refuge, especially as I encounter …
- I pray that … *(name)* will trust You as their refuge as they face …
- Lord, remind me that You see my heart, especially this next week as I …

READINESS – *Encouragement and strength for spiritual battle*

- Holy Lord, let us walk in Your righteousness, when wicked attacks tempt us to …
- Remind me that You love righteousness, especially when I encounter …

The upright will behold His face!

PSALM 12

Comments by Justin Jeppesen
Author David
Category Lament
In Brief The Lord's saving truth will prevail over all wicked lies and speech which seeks to bring harm to His people.

The words we speak are not mere vocalizations of thoughts, they have power to create realities. In this corporate song of lament, David despairingly describes a scene in his life where his enemies seem to be winning. Betrayal and lies were two things with which David was well acquainted. The faithful have vanished and the poor are oppressed by a generation marked by boastful speech and a prideful self-exaltation. A sense of helplessness has set in which explains the song's opening plea of desperation for the Lord to save. The succinct three-word prayer of "Save, O Lord" will always prove to be effective against a multitude of wicked rhetoric. When all allies have abandoned him and David is surrounded by prowling propaganda, God's truth still prevails. The dirty shell of lies, while seemingly powerful at first, will eventually be crushed by the weight of the pure words uttered by the mouth of the Lord. This Psalm can be broken into two parts. Part one (vv. 1-4) expounds upon the seedbed of lies that had contaminated the culture on every side. As David laments that faith and godly virtue have seemingly evaporated, he calls upon the Lord to bring His decisive judgment by "cutting off" the prideful lips of the wicked.

In part two (vv. 5-8) the deceptive sense that the boastful will prevail is strongly opposed. At just the right time, the Lord himself arises and speaks. His flawless words confront what is false. His perfect words reverse the trajectory of those who are being mistreated. The Lord's words are pure, which means they can be trusted. His pure words contain a promise of safety and protection that will guard his people forever. While this song closes with a lament that David's outward circumstances have not yet been resolved, God's word can, nevertheless, be trusted to bring about what He promises. Lastly, this Psalm points us to the example of Jesus, Who, despite suffering vile speech and evil false accusations, still found peace and strength by entrusting Himself to God's promises.

PSALM 12 – GUIDE

REVERENCE – *Identify and celebrate God's praiseworthy attributes*

- He saves – v. 1
- He cuts off the proud ("flattering lips") – vv. 3-4
- He provides safety for the poor and needy; His words are pure – vv. 5-6
- He protects His people from a godless generation – v. 7

Prayer Prompts
- I praise You that You can protect and save us even when . . .
- I praise You that You provided safety for me when . . .
- Because Your words are pure, they are able to . . .

RESPONSE – *Surrender to Him and His ways*

- In a world of godlessness, make me a godly example in my relationship with . . .
- Because faithfulness has vanished, give me grace to be faithful when . . .
- Because this world is filled with lies, I surrender to Your pure word today, trusting that it will produce … in me.

REQUESTS – *Ask the Spirit to guide your prayer over concerns, resources, and relationships*

- I pray for … *(name)* that You keep them safe in the midst of . . .
- I ask that Your pure word will work in me today so that I will . . .
- I pray that … *(name)* will embrace Your pure words as they face . . .
- Guard our children from … in the midst of a godless generation.

READINESS – *Encouragement and strength for spiritual battle*

- In this day, wickedness and vileness is pervasive, we trust You will guard us from . . .

Lead us not into temptation but deliver us from evil.

PSALM 13

Comments by Justin Jeppesen
Author   David
Category Lament
In Brief Waiting on God while in pain will eventually produce confidence and praise.

While this particular song of lament finds no specific backdrop in the life of David, it certainly alludes to numerous moments in his life. It reflects the inevitable experiences of any who seek God while living in the midst of a broken and fallen world. This Psalm seems to be clearly divided into three parts as it progresses from desperation, to supplication, to declaration.

The first two verses are densely packed with a striking honesty over the turmoil experienced while waiting on the Lord. The desperation can be heard by the fourfold cry of "How long?" A sense of anguish drips from David's cry. He is overtaken by sorrow, lamenting God's apparent distance. His enemy is closing in and he again seems helpless.

Yet desperation gives way to fervent supplication in verses 3 and 4. David makes it abundantly clear. Either the Lord steps in as his divine aid or he will die. The request assumes God's desire is to rescue and deliver David from his enemies. So he appeals to God's justice: "Do not allow the wicked to triumph over Your anointed king."

The last two verses move into a confident declaration that consoles the soul. David clings to God's character. His steadfast love, salvation and faithfulness will never fail. So David erupts in joyful praise. This Psalm draws our thoughts forward to Jesus as He waited on the Father in the Garden of Gethsemane, prayerfully progressing through the themes of this Psalm as He anticipated His own abandonment at Calvary.

Nevertheless, not My will, but Your will be done.

PSALM 13 – GUIDE

REVERENCE – *Identify and celebrate God's praiseworthy attributes*

- He listens to our questions and groanings – vv. 1-2
- Even when we doubt, He does not...
     Forget us or hide His face from us – v. 1
     Leave us in our sorrow or to our own counsel – v. 2
     Allow our enemies to triumph over us – v. 2
- He considers and answers us; He enlightens us; He fights for us – vv. 3-4
- He is a God of steadfast love Whose salvation brings joy – v. 5
- He is worthy of our song; He is good to us – v. 6

Prayer Prompts

- Thank You Lord that You have answered when I had questions about ...
- Thank You that I can trust in Your steadfast love, even when . . .
- I sing to You because You showed me Your goodness when . . .

RESPONSE – *Surrender to Him and His ways*

- Lord, I confess that my heart asks, "How Long?" when I think about ...
- Give me a deeper trust in You.

REQUESTS – *Ask the Spirit to guide your prayer over concerns, resources, and relationships*

- Lord, today I need Your light and steadfast love as I deal with . . .
- Give me Your joy today even though . . .
- Give Your light and life to ... *(name)* as they deal with . . .
- Show Your steadfast love to ... *(name)* in the midst of . . .
- I pray that ... *(name)* will know the joy of Your salvation as I seek to share the gospel.

READINESS – *Encouragement and strength for spiritual battle*

- God considers and answers when the enemy seeks to ...

We will not be shaken!

PSALM 14

Comments by Sandy Robertson
Author   David
Category Lament
In Brief The depravity and the activity of a world without God.

A highly educated atheist once challenged a simple Christian to a debate on the existence of God. The believer agreed but added one condition: "You must bring to the debate three witnesses who will testify that since they became an atheist, their life has been changed. Three who can say, 'Since I became an atheist, I no longer beat my wife and I don't get drunk, I now have a love for my neighbor that I never had before, and I have a deep peace and joy in my heart.'" The atheist would not agree to the condition so the debate was canceled.

What God Hears and Sees (vv. 1-3). Note that the fool's denial, "There is no God," comes from the heart, and not necessarily the mouth. God hears what we speak as well as what we think or imagine on the inside. We often read in the Gospels of the Lord Jesus responding to unspoken thoughts (Lu. 5:21-23; 7:39-40; 9:46-48). Most fools don't profess to be atheists. You would never hear God-denying words proceeding from their mouths. However, in practice, they are atheists. They live as though there was no God. Their thoughts are verbalized internally and manifested externally. A fool says ... there is no God, no afterlife, no accountability, no judgment. A fool says ... "No God for me ever" or "No God for me, at least not right now." A fool is ... someone who replaces God and His ways with self and his ways. A fool imagines ... a world with no God, no religion, no heaven, no hell. God looks down from heaven and sees nothing but corruption. There is no one who does good, not one. "All have sinned and fallen short of the glory of God" (Rom. 3:23). What a pandemic sin is ... this spiritual cancer that has infected the entire human race. The wise philosopher had it right, "The problem with the world is me." It is my heart that is "deceitful above all things and desperately wicked" (Jer. 17:9). It is me that needs to be changed. Salvation has come (v. 7).

Thankfully, a Savior has already come down from heaven to free us from sin and reconcile us back to God. His name is Jesus. Now, we are no longer "in this world without God" and "dead in our trespasses and sins." He has made us new. We have been given a fresh start.

PSALM 14 – GUIDE

REVERENCE – *Identify and celebrate God's praiseworthy attributes*
- He is in the heavens and sees all the affairs of men – v. 2
- He desires understanding and seeks those who will seek Him – v. 2
- He brings terror to the godless, but blesses the generation of the righteous – v. 5
- He is the refuge for the poor – v. 6
- He is salvation for His people; restores their blessing, gives gladness – v. 7

Prayer Prompts
- I praise You that You are in heaven and supreme above …
- Thank You that You have given me understanding about …
- Lord, You have put it in my heart to seek You because You are …
- I praise You that You were my refuge when …

RESPONSE – *Surrender to Him and His ways*

- I confess that I have been foolish when I have said "no" to You about …
- I surrender my feelings of … when I see the godlessness of this world.
- I confess that I failed to understand Your ways when …

REQUESTS – *Ask the Spirit to guide your prayer over concerns, resources, and relationships*

- Lord, today I need understanding as I …
- Lord, I pray that … *(name)* will trust You as their refuge as they….
- Lord, today I look to You to restore …
- Break through the unbelief of … *(name)* and cause them to seek You.
- In a world of foolishness, help me to know that You see and judge …

READINESS – *Encouragement and strength for spiritual battle*

- Because You are with the righteous, I will trust You to give me victory over …
- I will trust You as my refuge when the wicked try to …
- It will trust You to restore, save and give me joy especially when …

PSALM 15

Comments by Sandy Robertson
Author   David
Category Royal
In Brief Describes how Kingdom people live.

David asks the question, God gives the answer. Speaking on behalf of himself and all God-seekers, King David wants to know, "Who can live in God's Presence?" God responds by describing the character traits of the person who dwells with God. Entrance into His abode is granted to the man or woman who walks right and talks right. They love right. They hate wrong. They live faultless before both God and their fellow man.

Who can satisfy these righteous requirements? No one that I know of, and neither does David. In another place he confesses, "I was brought forth in iniquity and in sin my mother conceived me" (Ps. 51:5). No one lives like Psalm 15 requires, not fully.

But wait a minute. There was One who lived like the person described in verses 2-5. God said of Him, "This is my Beloved Son in whom I am well-pleased." His prosecutor said, "I find no fault in Him." Even an evil spirit said, "I know who You are, the Holy One of God." The Man Jesus Christ was perfect, blameless and without sin.

It is a good and godly desire to seek to dwell in God's presence, but there is one great obstacle that we all face: God is holy and we are not. Our sin has separated us from God. The door into His presence is closed. We need an Advocate. Someone with access. Someone who will speak on our behalf. Jesus has opened the way for us.

It matters Who you know.

PSALM 15 – GUIDE

REVERENCE – *Identify and celebrate God's praiseworthy attributes*

- He is Lord (YHWH), holy, and welcoming – v. 1
- He cares about and produces righteousness and blamelessness in us – v. 2
- He is a God of truth who brings truth to our very core – v. 2
- He is a God who transforms our relationships to reflect His character – vv. 3-4
- He is a God who cares about financial integrity; He is our stability – v. 5

Prayer Prompts

- Because You desire blamelessness, even though I used to … *(former behavior),* I experience Your holy presence and desire what is right.
- Because of Your truth, You empower me to speak the truth in my heart about…
- I thank You that because of Your … *(attribute)* You have changed my relationships.

RESPONSE – *Surrender to Him and His ways*

- Because I want to be blameless, do the right thing, and speak truth in my heart … I surrender to You and Your will, especially in my struggle with …

REQUESTS – *Ask the Spirit to guide your prayer over concerns, resources, and relationships*

- Give me grace today to restrain my tongue when I talk about … *(name or situation).*
- Give me grace to do good and not evil today in my interactions with …
- Give me grace to keep my commitments, especially in my relationship with …
- Give me grace today to honor You in how I spend and make my money *(as a visual reminder, take out your wallet and surrender it to the Lord)*

READINESS – *Encouragement and strength for spiritual battle*

- By Your truth and power, help me not be "moved/shaken" today, especially as I encounter …

PSALM 16

Comments by Sandy Robertson
Author   David
Category   Prophesy
In Brief   There is no substitute for His Presence.

How would you fill in the blank, "I would be content if I had _____?" You might answer … A good job. A better marriage. Financial security. Successful ministry. Peace of mind. Good health. Someone to share my life with. The list is endless. Ask David to fill in the blank and we know from this Psalm and several others that his response would be this: "I would be content if I had the Presence of God" (Ps 27:4, 8, Ps. 51:11).

David concludes Psalm 16 on this life-affirming note. "It's your Presence that fills me with joy" (v. 11). David is not alone in his pursuit of God's Presence. Moses, the emancipator of the children of Israel, boldly appeals to God, "If your Presence does not go with us, do not bring us up from here" (Ex. 33:15).

Hymn writer Frances Brook penned these God-pursuing words: "My Goal is God Himself, not joy, nor peace, nor even blessing, but Himself, my God; 'Tis His to lead me there—not mine, but His— at any cost, dear Lord, by any road." So faith bounds forward to its goal in God, and love can trust her Lord to lead her there; upheld by Him, my soul is following hard, till God hath fulfilled my deepest prayer."

In Luke 9:57, a potential Christ-follower impetuously declares, "Lord, I will follow You wherever You go." Jesus responds, "Foxes have holes, birds of the air have nests, but the Son of Man has nowhere to lay his head." He was effectively asking that man and all who would follow Him, "Am I sufficient? Will you be satisfied with Me alone and not just for what I can give you or do for you?"

Pastor Tripp calls what many want from God is a "Prozac Jesus." That is, someone who will make us feel good; someone who will make us happy, give us a little comfort and a bit of pleasure. That someone is not the God of the Bible.

If Christ is your Lord and Savior, God is not far from you. He dwells within your heart by His Spirit (1 Cor. 6:19). Find contentment in Him. Enjoy His Presence now and forevermore!

PSALM 16 – GUIDE

REVERENCE – *Identify and celebrate God's praiseworthy attributes*

- He preserves/keeps us safe, He is our refuge – v. 1
- He is our Lord/ruler and the source of goodness – v. 2
- He makes us His people/saints – v. 3
- He is our destiny and guarantee, He promises and provides inheritance – vv. 5-6
- He counsels/instructs; He is ever present and always near – vv. 7-8
- He is our stability/security and our joy – vv. 8-9
- He is our resurrection and the source of all pleasure – v. 10

Prayer Prompts

- I praise You that You were my … *(attribute)* when …
- I praise You that You recently revealed to me … *(attribute)*
- Because You are … *(attribute)* I am able to …

RESPONSE – *Surrender to Him and His ways*

- Because You preserve me and keep me safe, I surrender my fears about …
- Because You are my Lord, I confess my disobedience and rebellion about …
- I confess that I did not listen to Your counsel/instruction this week when …
- I confess that I settled for less than Your will/pleasure when …

REQUESTS – *Ask the Spirit to guide your prayer over concerns, resources, and relationships*

- Be my … as I face …
- I pray that You will show … *(name)* that You are their … in their trials.
- Help us as a church to trust You to … as we face …

READINESS – *Encouragement and strength for spiritual battle*

- Because You are (attribute), we trust You to help us live in victory over …

PSALM 17

Comments by S. Lindsay Taylor
Author   David
Category Lament
In Brief David feels like there is no one to protect him.

David is not complacent but is deeply concerned for integrity, both man's truth and God's. He continues in his battle with wicked men and expresses his deep concern for righteous judgment upon them. Who among us has not had similar feelings? David searches his heart before the Lord to find assurance of his own piety. Therefore, he appeals to God to judge the situation. The concern David has for righteousness dominates this Psalm, and, as a result, drives him to prayer. This prayer wrenches itself from the soul of a man hard pressed by deadly enemies, in a moment of great danger.

Though David begins with lament, there is a fantastic change of heart and mind as he seeks the Lord. His heart is refreshed and encouraged when he remembers that the Lord hears and answers prayer (v. 6). In this time of renewing, David is drenched in the lovingkindness of God (v. 7) and now knows once again, that he is "the apple of God's eye." This is the Psalm's encouragement: David is well regarded by God now, but he will see the face of God one day (v. 15) and be satisfied in and by Him.

May our satisfaction be in Christ and Christ alone. Not in any of the temporary works of this life that so easily captivate us. May we throw off the works of the flesh and be drawn into renewal as David was.

Look up, our redemption draws near! (Luke 21:28)

PSALM 17 – GUIDE

REVERENCE – *Identify and celebrate God's praiseworthy attributes*
- He hears and vindicates, sees and tests us – vv. 1-3
- His word strengthens and guides us; He answers our prayers – vv. 4 – 6
- He is a God of steadfast love, a refuge from our adversaries – v. 7
- He confronts our enemies and delivers us – v. 13
- He draws us to His righteous face; His presence satisfies – v. 15

Prayer Prompts
- Thank You that Your word strengthened and guided me when . . .
- I praise You that Your love is steadfast even when I . . .
- I praise You that You have delivered me from . . .
- Thank You that Your presence satisfies my need for . . .

RESPONSE – *Surrender to Him and His ways*

- Lord, as You test my heart, I know You find ... I surrender that to You.
- I confess that I often transgress with my mouth when ...
- I pray that Your Spirit would grant me self-control.
- I confess that my steps do not hold fast to Your path when ... Give me grace to not slip.

REQUESTS – *Ask the Spirit to guide your prayer over concerns, resources, and relationships*

- Hide me in the shadow of Your wings as I am in the midst of...
- Show Your steadfast love to ... *(name)* as they seek refuge in You.
- I pray for ... *(name)* as they trust in Your strong right hand in the midst of ...

READINESS – *Encouragement and strength for spiritual battle*

- Arise, O Lord, and confront the enemies of Your people as You ...
- I trust You to deliver me from the wickedness of the world when I ...
- Thank You that You are greater than the ambush of the enemy when he tempts me to ...

PSALM 18

Comments by S. Lindsay Taylor
Author David
Category Thanksgiving
In Brief A song of praise, thanksgiving, and victory by the servant of the Lord.

Psalm 18 can be summarized in one verse. In verse 2 David uses multiple images to declare his sustained reliance on God. "My Rock!" Visualize an immense boulder that is part of an amazing castle. This is a place of great protection and security. It is a picturesque way to convey that God is secure, stable, and unchangeable—the One David knew he could always count on.

"My fortress" compares God to a fortified, natural stronghold signifying protection and safety in the most profound way. A hand-held shield provides some protection, but nothing like that of a fortress! David had found that place of true security, which exists in God alone.

"Deliverer" means "one who rescues or liberates." David knew that God had not only rescued him from his physical enemies, but also from afflictions and temptations. He was David's shield, his protection not only from those who pursued him, but also from the fiery darts of his spiritual enemy.

"Horn of my salvation" is a metaphor relating to horned beasts that push, scatter, and destroy their enemies; David knew that God was his Savior and the One who could and would triumph over every foe.

"High tower" pictures a place of refuge far out of the reach of any who would attempt harm. Though David was at the height of his royal dominion at the time of this writing, he referred to himself as "the servant of the Lord" and took no glory for himself. Rather, he focused entirely on joyful praise for God's power and majesty. He would overcome all!

Like David, we can have absolute confidence in our all-powerful God. He is our unfailing place of refuge, strength and security!

PSALM 18 – GUIDE

REVERENCE – *Identify and celebrate God's praiseworthy attributes*
- Our strength, rock, fortress, deliverer, refuge, shield, salvation, and stronghold
- He is deserving of our love and worthy of our praise and song – vv. 1, 3, 49
- He hears our cries for help when we are in distress – vv. 4-6
- He demonstrates His power in nature – vv. 7-15
- He draws us out of trouble and rescues us from strong enemies – vv. 16-17, 19
- He blesses our obedience and rewards His people's character – vv. 20-26
- He saves the humble and humbles the proud – v. 27
- He is our light in darkness, He empowers us and is perfect and true – vv. 28-30
- The one and only Lord God and the source of all greatness – vv. 31, 35, 43, 46
- He equips us with strength for the battles of life – vv. 32, 34, 39
- He makes our way blameless, perfect, and safe – vv. 32-33
- He is the source of all greatness – vv. 35, 43
- He overcomes and delivers us from our enemies – vv. 37-45, 47-48
- He shows His steadfast love forever – v. 50

Prayer Prompts
- Lord, I love You because …
- Lord, I witnessed Your power over nature when …
- Thank You, Lord, that Your word proved true in my life when …

RESPONSE – *Surrender to Him and His ways*
- Because You desire righteousness and clean hands, I confess …
- You save a humble people, I surrender my pride in the area of …
- Your word is proven true, I commit to obey You when You say …

REQUESTS – *Ask the Spirit to guide your prayer over concerns, resources, and relationships*
- Today, as I am in distress about … I call upon You to help me.
- Today I am trusting in Your perfect ways and true word as I deal with …
- I pray for … *(name)* in their time of distress. Please help them to …
- Thank You that You are our security, especially when the world …

READINESS – *Encouragement and strength for spiritual battle*
- We trust You to save us from the enemy of …
- Lord, be our light as we encounter the darkness of …

Your word is perfect and proven true!

PSALM 19

Comments by S. Lindsay Taylor
Author   David
Category Thanksgiving
In Brief A declaration of the glory of the Lord through His self-revelation in creation and in His law.

Many commentators suggest that this is one of the most magnificent of the Psalms, both for its poetic elegance and its theological depth. Its theme is that there can be no excuse for those who do not believe in God's existence, for God has revealed Himself to mankind through His creation and through His Word.

For many years I pastored a wonderful church in northern Alberta. The glory of the night sky when the northern lights would dance come to mind every time I think on this Psalm. The first portion of the Psalm, (vv. 1-6), uses the example of the heavens to illustrate that creation serves as a witness to God's existence. The Apostle Paul would tell the Roman church that no one has an excuse before God because of this general revelation.

Verses 7-14 turn from the glory of God apparent in nature, to the glory of God revealed in His Word. Five synonyms for the Word of God are given in these verses: the "law of the Lord," the "testimony," the "statutes," the "commandment," and the "judgments."

David made eight statements about the Word of God: it is perfect, it is sure, it is right, it is pure, it is clean, it is true and righteous, and it is of infinite value. David may also have been emphasizing the sufficiency of God's Word for us.

The Psalm ends with a prayer. In verses 12 and 13, David asked God to cleanse him from "hidden faults" and "presumptuous sins." He concludes with a plea that his words and the meditations of his heart would be "acceptable" to God. As we wonder at His creation and read His Word, may that be our heart today!

PSALM 19 – GUIDE

REVERENCE – *Identify and celebrate God's praiseworthy attributes*

- Glorious, Creator, Revealer of Truth – vv. 1-6
- Your Word is…
    - Perfect, life giving, sure, wise – v. 7
    - Right, joyful, pure, enlightening – v. 8
    - To be feared, eternal, truth, righteous – v. 9
    - Our ultimate treasure and pleasure – v. 10
    - Guide, rewarder, knows our hearts and declares us innocent – vv. 11-12
    - Delivers from sin, makes blameless – v. 13
    - Our rock and redeemer – v. 14

Prayer Prompts

- Lord, thank You that we have witnessed Your glory in creation when …
- Your creation declares that You are … and so will we be.
- Your word is able to… and more valuable than …

RESPONSE – *Surrender to Him and His ways*

- I confess that I have often desired … more than Your word.
- I trust that You will deliver/keep me back from the sin of …
- I acknowledge that my words and thoughts were not acceptable to You when …

REQUESTS – *Ask the Spirit to guide your prayer over concerns, resources, and relationships*

- I trust that You will revive my soul so that I will …
- I need Your wisdom today as I …
- I pray that the truth of Your word will produce righteousness in me so that …

READINESS – *Encouragement and strength for spiritual battle*

- I pray that I will obey the warning of Your word when I face …
- Remind me of the reward of obedience to Your word when the enemy tempts me to …
- Give me grace to trust You as my Rock and Redeemer when the enemy seeks to …

PSALM 20

Comments by Mike Moran
Author   David
Category   Royal
In Brief   In faith, Israel's King David cries out to God, asking for His provision during crisis.

It is quite possible that this song would have been sung to the Lord before going to battle, as the people gathered to ask God for what only He can do. Anticipating an upcoming conflict would certainly cause distress in those preparing to go, their families who remain behind, and the entire community. David directs those who might be distressed to look up, into the Name of the One who can bring hope and relief to their distress. He points to the God who protects, helps, and provides support to those He loves. David is sure of God's answer. And the singing of this song must have uplifted the spirit of those singing, while readying them for battle. While their opponents might trust in their weapons for war, David declares their trust is in the Lord alone!

The role of a spiritual leader is to keep pointing people upward, to the One who created and sustains all that is. David, despite his own personal and political problems or shortfalls, remains faithful to this aspect of his leadership. He could have responded in so many varied ways. Yet again, he leads in faith and brings needed perspective to the people. We can do the same!

PSALM 20 – GUIDE

REVERENCE – *Identify and celebrate God's praiseworthy attributes*

- God protects us by His Name and answers us in our troubles – vv. 1, 6, 9
- Regards our sacrifices; grants our desires – vv. 3-4
- Grants joyful salvation and victory in His name – vv. 5-6
- His name is trustworthy – v. 7
- Gives us power to stand, He is mighty – vv. 8-9

Prayer Prompts

- I praise You Lord that You answered me in trouble when …
- I praise You for the joy I feel because You saved me from …
- Because Your name is … I can trust You for …
- Thank You that You give us power to stand, even when we encounter …

RESPONSE – *Surrender to Him and His ways*

- I surrender my heart's desire for … conform it to Your will.
- I submit my plans for … direct my steps to honor You.
- I confess that too often, rather than trusting in Your name, I have put my trust in …

REQUESTS – *Ask the Spirit to guide your prayer over concerns, resources, and relationships*

- Today, I call on Your name to help me as I …
- I pray that we will know the shout of joy when You save … *(name)* from …
- Lord, I pray that You would give divine support to … *(name)* as they …
- We call on You to save our spiritual leaders from …

READINESS – *Encouragement and strength for spiritual battle*

- Thank You that Your name is our banner of victory over the enemy of …

We shout for joy in Your salvation!

PSALM 21

Comments by Mike Moran

Author   David

Category   Royal

In Brief   David returns from battle praising God and giving Him credit for success against his enemies, past, present, and future.

David gives thanks to God for a recent victory, previously referred to in Psalm 20, describing specifically how the Lord brought about this victory through answered prayer and abundant blessing. Isn't it critically important, when God brings victory, that we take time to stop, reflect, and respond in thanksgiving and praise? If we fail to do so, it becomes only too easy to take the credit for what God has brought about. Nothing makes one's celebration following victory the best it can be than by celebrating and speaking about God's protective actions taken on our behalf!

He then speaks about his enemies, emphasizing confidence in God's ongoing protection and rescue from their schemes. It would have been easy for David to seek vengeance against those who sought to take his life, but he chooses the better way. What a great life lesson for us! Think about those who oppose you, who are against you, and instead of thinking poorly of them, entrust them to the Lord and His activity in their lives. What an opportunity to practice Jesus' teaching regarding our enemies, to love them, to pray for them, to entrust them into God's hand. What a difference this would make in our lives!

PSALM 21 – GUIDE

REVERENCE – *Identify and celebrate God's praiseworthy attributes*
- He is our God, even when we feel He is far away and silent – vv. 1-2
- He is Holy, King, and worthy of our trust – vv. 3-5
- He delivers and rescues – vv. 4, 5, 20, 21
- He is our God before and after our birth – vv. 9-10
- He is our present help in trouble – vv. 11, 19
- His word predicted the sufferings of Christ – vv. 12-18

Prayer Prompts
- Lord, You are Holy because You are …
- I praise You that You are enthroned above …
- I thank You that You have shown Your trustworthiness in the past when …
- I praise You that You have delivered and rescued me from …

RESPONSE – *Surrender to Him and His ways*
- I confess that I felt forsaken by You when … but declare now that You are truly my God.
- My soul found no rest when I … but You have always been my faithful deliverer.
- I confess that my soul is sometimes troubled when the ungodly despise my faith and mock Your name. Help me to trust You even when …

REQUESTS – *Ask the Spirit to guide your prayer over concerns, resources, and relationships*
- Help me to know that You are a holy, trustworthy and rescuing God, even when I feel …
- Lord, today, I trust You to deliver me from …
- I pray for … *(name)* whose soul is restless. Reveal Your rescuing power to them today.
- I pray for … *(name)* that they will cry out to You, and that You will rescue them from …
- I pray for our church as we face … Help us and come quickly to our aid.

READINESS – *Encouragement and strength for spiritual battle*
- Even though the attacks of our enemy can feel like … we know You will deliver us.
- You are able to deliver, save and rescue us from … *(attack/evil)*

You are our help! Come quickly to our aid.

PSALM 22

Comments by Mike Moran
Author David
Category Prophesy
In Brief Written one thousand years before Jesus' arrival, Psalm 22 describes, with amazing accuracy, not only David's plight but Messiah's future experience on the cross, followed by a beautiful description of the outcome of His sacrifice.

David is once again crying out to God for help. He is being opposed and ridiculed on all sides. His enemies mock him because His God seems uninterested in his current troubles. To David it seems as though God is far off, unconcerned, and uninvolved in his plight. He then begins to re-count God's faithfulness throughout time, as though contrasting or maybe even complaining about what he is currently experiencing. In one paragraph he complains about his circumstances and then in the next applauds God's faithfulness. We've all been there, haven't we?

In verse 19, David's focus changes from his problems to God's providence. You can almost sense the attitude and emotional changes as he writes. No more complaining, no more detailing of his troubles, but an obvious upward movement regarding the true nature and activity of His God. David has chosen to set his mind, heart, and soul on what he knows to be true about God instead of how he might be feeling mentally or emotionally.

One can't miss the futuristic, prophetic nature of Psalm 22. Not only does the Psalm describe David's plight, but it also predicts the suffering of the One who would come to redeem humanity from the destructive nature of sin, granting forgiveness to everyone who believes. Jesus' final hours on earth are described so exactly in verses 14-18 that one would have to work hard to suppress the truth that Jesus is found in this ancient text. Psalm 22 has been so important in helping people, throughout the ages, to connect the dots regarding Old Testament prophecy and the revelation of the Messiah, finding life eternal in His Name.

PSALM 22 – GUIDE

REVERENCE – *Identify and celebrate God's praiseworthy attributes*
- He is our God, He is Holy; He is there and worthy of our trust – vv. 1-3, 9-10
- He is our helper in troubles and rescues us – vv. 11, 19-21
- His word predicted the sufferings of Christ – vv. 12-18
- He is awesome, He is our life and worthy of praise – vv. 22-26
- He sees and hears us in our afflictions – v. 24
- He rules as King and will be worshiped by all nations – vv. 27-29
- He is righteous, His truth enduring to all generations – vv. 29-31

Prayer Prompts
- I praise Your trustworthiness because …
- We stand in awe of You because …
- Thank You that You were with me in … and rescued me when …
- We praise You that You rule as King over …

RESPONSE – *Surrender to Him and His ways*
- I confess that I often fear and reverence … more than I do You.
- I remember my soul found no rest when … But You have always been faithful.
- King Jesus, rule over my life today, especially …

REQUESTS – *Ask the Spirit to guide your prayer over concerns, resources, and relationships*
- Hear my cry today as I seek You for …
- I pray for … *(name)* in this time of difficulty. Let them find their satisfaction in You.
- Give me strength to keep my commitments to You in …
- I pray for our church as we face … Help us and come quickly to our aid.
- Lord Jesus, I pray for Your rule over our nation, especially …
- For those in the nation of … *(name),* may they turn to You and believe Your gospel.

READINESS – *Encouragement and strength for spiritual battle*
- Even though the attacks of the enemy can feel like … You will deliver our souls.
- King Jesus, help us proclaim Your righteousness to the coming generations, especially when they …

PSALM 23

Comments by Mike Mitchener
Author David
Category Confidence
In Brief The Great Shepherd provides for and protects His sheep.

Psalm 23 is one of the best-known passages in all of Scripture; perhaps because it is so commonly read at funerals. The Lord has used David's words to comfort those mourning the loss of a loved one through the ages. He has done so for me and He most likely has done so for you too.

However, we must never forget that the LORD gave us Psalm 23 for our day-to-day lives. In it He reminds us that amid our daily toils and struggles, He is providing, restoring, leading, comforting, anointing, and blessing us all day, every day.

The foundational truth that gives Psalm 23 such power is expressed in the heart of verse 4: *"for You are with me."* The LORD is with me whether I am resting in green pastures or among my enemies, in the house of the Lord or in the shadow of death. He wants me to remember His presence is with me all my days (and He has great purpose for every day).

So, wherever you are right now, even in the valley of the shadow of death itself –lay down and rest easy in the great Shepherd's watchful care. God's goodness and mercy are all around you today, because He is all around you today. Just open your eyes and look for Him, today.

> *LORD, open my eyes to see Your goodness and mercy, Your provisions and protection, Your anointing and blessings in the midst of my day.*

Psalm 23 – Guide

REVERENCE – *Identify and celebrate God's praiseworthy attributes*

- He is Shepherd, Provider, and Peace Giver vv. 1-2
- Glorious Restorer and Comforter vv. 3-4
- Abundant Giver, Good and merciful promise keeper vv. 4-6

Prayer Prompts
- I praise You Good Shepherd, that You cared for me when …
- I praise You that You led me to … when I …
- You give me peace even when …

RESPONSE – *Surrender to Him and His ways*

- Lord, I surrender my desire to have … realizing that You provide all I need.
- You are the leader, so I surrender my self-made plans for …
- Though I will be with You forever, I confess I often try to find value in …

REQUESTS – *Ask the Spirit to guide your prayer over concerns, resources, and relationships*

- I pray that … *(name)* will find satisfaction in You and not in …
- Lord, I am trusting You to restore …
- Lord, I call on Your name to lead as I …
- I pray that I will have a firm assurance of Your goodness as I …

READINESS – *Encouragement and strength for spiritual battle*

- Even though we walk through … *(difficulty)* we will fear no evil.
- You are our provision, even in the presence of … *(various forms of evil).*

Our cup overflows! You are with us!

PSALM 24

Comments by Mike Mitchener
Author   David
Category   Praise
In Brief   Who is this King of glory?

My daughter-in-law delivered our first grandchild five weeks pre-mature. We could not hold him, we could only gaze through the incubator at his sweet little face. When the time came for us to finally get to hold him the hospital made us thoroughly cleanse ourselves and don sterile garments. We did not hesitate to do so. (And this was pre-COVID 19!) We knew a thorough scrubbing was the only way we would be able to enter our grandson's presence. Once in the NICU room, we spent hours staring at his face. It awakened in us a deep and powerful love we had never experienced, even in our relationships with our children (which we also love dearly). We did not want to leave the room.

The LORD wants a whole generation of followers to seek His face, to desire to be in His presence even more than we desired to be in our grandson's presence. But to do so, we must follow His rules. We must cleanse ourselves first. When we scrubbed to see my grandson, we did so thoroughly; we did not want to miss anything. Yet, we often try to approach God without "scrubbing" spiritually. Ask His Holy Spirit to convict you of *any* sin lingering in your heart. Only with clean hands and a pure heart can you ascend the hill of the Lord, His Holy Place, and enter the presence of this King of glory. Trust me, once you enter His throne-room, you will not want to leave.

Father, I want to seek Your face, but first, I must confess the sin of _____. Thank You for cleansing my hand and purifying my heart so I can enter Your presence.

PSALM 24 – GUIDE

REVERENCE – *Identify and celebrate God's praiseworthy attributes*
- He is Creator and Master, Founder and Sustainer of all creation – vv. 1-2
- He is Holy and worthy of pure worship – vv. 3-4
- He is our Rewarder and Vindicator; He is worthy to be sought – vv. 5-6
- The King of Glory, mighty and majestic; the Lord of armies – vv. 7-10

Prayer Prompts
- I praise You that You are the creator and master of …
- You are absolutely holy and unaffected by this world's …
- Thank You that, in Christ, I have received the blessing of …
- I praise You that when I seek Your face, I see …
- Lord of hosts, I praise You that You rule over …

RESPONSE – *Surrender to Him and His ways*
- I confess that I do not worship You from a pure heart, especially when …
- I confess my tendency to be deceitful when … Cleanse and empower me in truth and give me grace to make this right with others.
- King of Glory, I open my life to Your rule once again and surrender my …

REQUESTS – *Ask the Spirit to guide your prayer over concerns, resources, and relationships*
- Help my worship to be pure and true today so that …
- I pray that … *(name)* will receive the blessing and righteousness of Your salvation by turning to Christ in true faith and worship.
- Teach us to seek Your face so that we …
- Because You are strong and mighty, I trust You to …
- King of Glory, in my life (see 2 Cor. 4:6), enable me to glorify You when …

READINESS – *Encouragement and strength for spiritual battle*
- Because You are mighty in battle, work in the life of … *(name)* to win their battle with …
- Because You are mighty in battle, give us victory over …

Lord of Hosts! King of Glory!

PSALM 25

Comments by Mike Mitchener
Author   David
Category   Confidence
In Brief   Petition for protection, guidance and pardon.

I became a follower of Jesus Christ in my mid-twenties. I had plenty of time to realize how sinful I was at the core of my being. Like David, I knew I was totally corrupt and depraved. You can imagine the relief in my soul when I realized the all-knowing Lord (that knew about every one of my sins) said, *"Mike, I am not going to remember you by the sins of your youth. Instead, I am going to remember you according to My loyal love for you."* Wow!

He does not remember me the same way *I* remember me. He consciously chooses to remember me through the lens of His nature, not mine, including His faithfulness, love, mercy, and forgiveness. Just as amazing is that He pardons my guilt for *His good*, not just mine (v. 11). It brings Him glory as He demonstrates His ability to redeem me *and* my past.

He is working everything for His good and His glory. My life is all about Him! My job today is to keep my eyes ever focused on Him and His glory. As the beneficiary of such an overwhelming "friendship," I can do nothing but drop to my knees in humble adoration as joy replaces the shame in my soul. And then get up and live each day of my life knowing that God has a plan, and I can trust it.

What about the sins of your youth bring you the most shame? If you have accepted God's offer of salvation in Jesus Christ, you are forgiven, You are set free, you are redeemed out of your troubles. Praise the Lord, right!?

"Lord, I praise You that You remember me according to Your steadfast love. You have pardoned and redeemed my past. I praise You that You have forgiven me for Your name's sake, for Your good and mine. Thank You for replacing my shame with joy. I am forgiven.

PSALM 25 – GUIDE

REVERENCE – *Identify and celebrate God's praiseworthy attributes*
- Our God provides rest for the weary and oppressed soul – vv. 1-3, 16-20
- He is a wise teacher and the One who saves – vv. 4-5
- He is proven compassionate and faithful – v. 5
- Good and willing to forgive sinners – vv. 7-8
- One who gives grace and guidance to the humble – vv. 9, 12, 14
- Intimate with us in revealing His heart – v. 14
- Mighty to save, our refuge, guard, Savior and Redeemer– vv. 16-22

Prayer Prompts
- I praise You, Sovereign One, that You are able to give me rest even in the midst of …
- Thank You that even now You are working to save me from …
- I praise You for Your mercy and steadfast love, evidenced in …
- Thank You for being my refuge when …

RESPONSE – *Surrender to Him and His ways*
- I trust You to fulfill Your purposes for me, even in the midst of …
- I confess that my sins are many …
- I confess that my soul at times is not well for I fear … more than I fear You.
- My tendency is pride when … give grace to make this right with others.

REQUESTS – *Ask the Spirit to guide your prayer over concerns, resources, and relationships*
- Because You are a wise Father, give me guidance for …
- I pray that … *(name)* will receive the blessing and righteousness of Your salvation
- Because You are sovereign and mighty, I trust You to …
- Help me to extend Your mercy, grace and forgiveness to … *(name)*.

READINESS – *Encouragement and strength for spiritual battle*
- As I wait for You, let me not be put to shame in …
- Be my refuge from … today.
- Deliver … *(name)* from the work of the enemy today.

PSALM 26

Comments by Jon Hoekema

Author   David

Category   Lament

In Brief   A prayer for God's protection and redemption where David asks God to acknowledge and protect his integrity.

David finds himself in the crosshairs of his enemies once again. These deceitful (v. 4) and bloodthirsty (v. 9) men are coming after him and David cries out to God for vindication – a cry for justice in the midst of injustice.

David's appeal is for God to vindicate him because of his life of integrity. While David is certainly not a perfect man, he is known as a man after God's own heart (1 Samuel 13:14, Acts 13:22), yet what makes him blameless is not perfection, but rather his putting his trust in the Lord. It is his understanding of who God is and his awareness of his own sinfulness and dependence upon God for grace, mercy, and love.

In his cry, David tells God to test and examine him. He is confident he will pass that testing because he keeps his eyes on God's love. The Hebrew word for "love", "steadfast love" or "loving kindness" (v. 3) is *hesed*. The word describes God's fierce loyalty, faithfulness, and commitment to His people. David's hope and security are not based on his works, on his blameless life, on his unwavering trust (v. 1) or God-honoring behavior (vv. 4-5) but on God's fierce loyalty and faithfulness to His people. David's blamelessness is through his trust and dependence upon the fierce loyalty of God.

With praise (v. 8) and trust (v. 12), David's firm conviction is in the confidence that God will protect and keep him, even though the outcome is uncertain. In the uncertain times in our lives, we can hold onto the *hesed* of God which holds onto us. Our hope and security are in God's faithfulness to His people, ultimately demonstrated in Jesus Christ. The result for us is being seen as without fault and filled with great joy in His presence (Jude 24-25).

PSALM 26 – GUIDE

REVERENCE – *Identify and celebrate God's praiseworthy attributes*

- God is sovereign judge – vv. 1, 9
- He is loving, loyal, and faithful – v. 3
- He is righteous, just, pure, and holy – vv. 4-7, 9-10
- He is our relational redeemer, gracious and glorious – vv. 8, 11

Prayer Prompts

- I praise You that You are sovereign over and involved in …
- Thank You for vindicating me when …
- Your steadfast love and faithfulness, evidenced in …
- Thank You for redeeming and giving me Your grace in …

RESPONSE – *Surrender to Him and His ways*

- As vindicator of Your people, I trust You to deliver me, even in the midst of …
- While committed to pleasing You, I confess I am a sinner, in Your grace …
- Lord, make me aware of any sin of which I am unaware so I may repent …

REQUESTS – *Ask the Spirit to guide your prayer over concerns, resources, and relationships*

- Give me grace to trust You unwaveringly in …
- May I trust You who judges justly when …
- Teach me to fear You above all, so that …
- Please redeem … *(name or circumstance)*

READINESS – *Encouragement and strength for spiritual battle*

- As I wait for You, do not let me be put to shame in …
- Grant me to maintain a posture of worship in the midst of …
- Deliver … *(name)* from the work of the enemy today.

PSALM 27

Comments by Jon Hoekema
Author   David
Category Confidence
In Brief Amid challenge and uncertainty, the Lord is our strength as
we seek His presence in our life.

David begins (vv. 1-3) and ends (vv. 13-14) Psalm 27 declaring trust in
the goodness of God amid attacks from his enemies. He seeks God's
presence (vv. 4-6) in His temple and deliverance (vv. 7-12) from those who
seek to destroy him.

The contrast between David's confidence in God and his pleas for deliverance may raise a question: How can David plea for deliverance and at
the same time testify to the confidence that God will save him? The answer:
David realizes that though he faces his enemies (v. 12) and feels abandoned
by his family (v. 10), it is God who holds him. We see that same quiet confidence with the Apostle Paul who writes about contentment in Philippians
4:11-12. For Paul, the security that comes through Jesus Christ gave him
confidence and contentment even when imprisoned.

David's desire amid his challenges was to be closer to God. The one
thing that he asks and seeks is that he may dwell in the place of God (v. 4).
And he repeats that desire when he writes, "Your face, Lord, I will seek" (v.
8) and "teach me Your ways, O Lord" (v. 11). His driving passion is that God
would be present with him.

When we face dark times in our lives, we can confidently say with David, "the Lord is my light and my salvation – whom shall I fear?" And we can
say with confidence, "I will see the goodness of the Lord." So we can take
heart and wait for the Lord.

PSALM 27 – GUIDE

REVERENCE – *Identify and celebrate God's praiseworthy attributes*
- Our light, salvation, and stronghold – vv. 1, 9
- Our confidence and protector – vv. 2-3
- He is beautiful, our shelter and sustainer – vv. 4-5
- Worthy of sacrifice and joyful praise – v. 6
- He hears and graciously answers; He is worthy – vv. 7-8
- He is faithful and present: He is righteously angry – vv. 9-10
- Our teacher Who leads us into strength and courage – vv. 11-14

Prayer Prompts
- I praise You that Your light is greater than the darkness of …
- I praise You that You are my stronghold, I do not have to fear …
- Lord, You are beautiful to me because …
- I shout for joy because …
- I praise You that I saw Your goodness when …

RESPONSE – *Surrender to Him and His ways*
- I confess the I am often fearful about… Renew me in the truth of Who You are.
- Rather than the "one thing" of Your beauty, I confess I often desire …
- I confess that when You call me to seek Your face, I sinfully seek … instead.

REQUESTS – *Ask the Spirit to guide your prayer over concerns, resources, and relationships*
- Because You are their stronghold, deliver … *(name)* from their fear of …
- Help me trust Your sheltering care when I am troubled about …
- Lord, hear my prayer as I trust You for… and be gracious to me.
- Lord, today, be my teacher and help me to learn that …

READINESS – *Encouragement and strength for spiritual battle*
- Lord, as I face a hostile world, I trust You to lead me so that I will …
- Because You are our Light and Salvation we will not fear …
- We will trust in Your goodness even when …

Be strong and take courage! Wait on the Lord!

PSALM 28

Comments by Jon Hoekema
Author   David
Category Lament
In Brief   Trusting in God's protection for recompense against and deliverance from enemies.

Once again, David cries out to God. He reminds God that He is his Rock and if He doesn't act, then David has no chance. David acknowledges that his only place for help in distress is God himself (v. 2). God is our security and the only one to whom we can truly turn. As followers of Jesus, it is on Christ, the solid rock that we stand.

The cry for God's justice against the evil doers is that they would be repaid for what they have done (v. 4). It is not so much just for their evil deeds as for being two-faced hypocrites, and having an utter disdain for the salvation of God (v. 5) and no use for God himself.

Thousands of years later, and the story is still the same. People say one thing to someone's face and something else when they're not there. They post something on social media that they wouldn't say if the person was in front of them. And people have an utter disdain and contempt for God. This is no surprise. Jesus says in John 15:18, "If the world hates you, keep in mind that it hated me first."

David turns to God and praises Him for his deliverance, that He is his strength and shield. As a result of knowing God, David has confidence in His help. Jesus is our ever-present help amid the brokenness and pain in this world (Ps 46:1-3). Our goal is not to avoid it nor escape it, but to hold on to God when it comes.

David declares that God is not just a fortress for him only, but a strength for His people everywhere and at all times. It is God who carries His people and protects and keeps them. The God who makes covenants with His people keeps His promises.

When you find yourself struggling or under attack from those hostile to God, be encouraged and strengthened that God hears your cry. He will be your shepherd and will carry you forever.

PSALM 28 – GUIDE

REVERENCE – *Identify and celebrate God's praiseworthy attributes*

- He is our rock and help, the Holy One who hears and is merciful – vv. 1-2, 6-7
- He judges the wicked – vv. 4-5
- Our trustworthy strength and shield, our refuge – vv. 7-8
- Our blessed Shepherd – v. 9

Prayer Prompts

- I praise You that You are my rock of stability and strength when …
- I praise You that Your sanctuary is Holy because You are …
- I praise You that You are my strength – stronger than …
- I praise You that You are a shield for … (name) as they encounter …
- My Shepherd, You carried me through …

RESPONSE – *Surrender to Him and His ways*

- Give me grace to experience genuine peace in my heart when …
- I confess that I am struggling to trust You for… Help my heart to trust completely.

REQUESTS – *Ask the Spirit to guide your prayer over concerns, resources, and relationships*

- I pray that You will extend saving mercy to … (name) in drawing them to Yourself.
- I pray You will strengthen my heart as I trust You for …
- I pray that You will bless … (name) and save them from …
- Help us trust You to be the Shepherd of our church as You carry us through …

READINESS – *Encouragement and strength for spiritual battle*

- When the wicked disregard Your works, give us strength to demonstrate that You are …
- We will trust You as our strength and shield when we face …
- Be our saving refuge when the enemy tries to …

Save Your people! Bless Your heritage!

PSALM 29

Comments by Aaron Telecky

Author   David
Category   Praise
In Brief   As the author of all creation, God is worthy of our worship and praise.

"Ascribe" (vv. 1-2) isn't a word most of us use very often, but it's a good word, especially in the way David employs it. Here he is urging us to freely give God the glory He is due. In verses 3-9, he explains why. "Look around at creation," he says, "because it doesn't matter where you are – atop the Rocky Mountains, wading along the ocean shore or hiking through a dense forest – His creative power is on display everywhere." "And," David adds, "that is over and above Him making it for our enjoyment."

Creation is a testimony to His incomparable greatness. He did it so that people everywhere would hear His voice and turn to Him. Simply put, creation declares, "Our God is an awesome God!" And as the old hymn says, whenever we as believers recognize "His power throughout the universe displayed," we should either rise to our feet or fall to our knees in wonder, ascribing to the Lord the glory due His name.

So as you go through this day, make time to look for God's glory in creation, whether in the majesty of rolling hills or the intricacy of a single flower and let it serve as one more reminder that the One who is capable of such wonderful creative works is more than able to take care of you. "The Lord will give strength to His people; the Lord will bless His people with peace" (v. 11).

PSALM 29 – GUIDE

REVERENCE – *Identify and celebrate God's praiseworthy attributes*

- He is awesome, glorious, mighty and worthy of praise – vv. 1-2, 4-5
- He rules and sustains the whole earth – vv. 3-9
- He is glorious and eternal; He is our strength and peace – vv. 9-11

Prayer Prompts

- God, I praise You for Your awesome might and majesty displayed in …
- Thank You, Lord, for sustaining me when …
- I praise You that You are sovereign over and involved in …
- Thank You for counting me among Your people, so that I may …

RESPONSE – *Surrender to Him and His ways*

- Your awesome power makes me feel …
- Lord I love Your glory because … I confess that I often …
- God, because You are above all, I surrender … afresh and anew to You today.

REQUESTS – *Ask the Spirit to guide your prayer over concerns, resources, and relationships*

- Father, nothing is impossible for You! Therefore, I ask …
- Teach me to fear You above all, so that …
- Lord, give strength to the relationship between … *(name and name)* right now, so that …
- Father, please bless … *(name)* with peace as they face … this week.

READINESS – *Encouragement and strength for spiritual battle*

- Lord, as I wait for You, please give me peace about …
- Father, may Your peace reign supreme in the … *(name's)* home this week.
- God, as I face … please grant me strength to fight the good fight of faith, so that …
- Father, let me ascribe to You the glory due Your Name, even in the midst of …

PSALM 30

Comments by Aaron Telecky
Author   David
Category   Thanksgiving
In Brief   A song of renewed joy in response to answered prayer.

As Christians, we're commonly reminded that the Lord doesn't always answer our prayers the way we wish. But oftentimes He does, and when His answer to us is "yes," we must do what David does here in Psalm 30: we must rejoice and sing praise to God! Take a moment to review what David specifically expressed gratitude for here: victory over enemies (v. 1), physical healing (v. 2), rescue from death and perhaps also depression (v. 3), and the experience of walking through a season of deep sorrow that eventually gave way to an even deeper sense of joy (v. 5). How has the Lord done that for you? What answers to prayer can you recount and turn into your own declarations of praise? If you have walked with Jesus for long at all, there are certainly going to be many.

Now there are several good reasons for us to recall answered prayers, one of which David mentions in vv. 6-9 – because we so easily forget! The sequence goes something like this: The Lord brings us through one of life's many trials. Life, then, returns more or less to "normal." Then, out of nowhere, another difficulty comes along and knocks us off balance. Despite the fact that we know better, we wonder, "What is God up to?" all over again. But then, once again, He graciously hears our cry, comes to our aid and restores our joy. *Again* (vv. 10-12).

So if today you're in a season of blessing, praise Him for it with your whole heart. If you aren't, take courage and have faith, because He has not forgotten you. In Christ, a day is coming when you will be able to rejoice again.

PSALM 30 – GUIDE

REVERENCE – *Identify and celebrate God's praiseworthy attributes*

- God is our deliverer, healer and helper – vv. 1-3
- Hears our cry – vv. 1, 8, 10
- He is holy and worthy of praise and thanks – vv. 4, 12
- Enduring in favor/grace and joy giver – v. 5
- Imparts strength/stability without which we cannot stand – v. 7
- Faithfully hears our cries and is merciful – vv. 8-10
- Imparts gladness and calls forth thanksgiving – vv. 11-12

Prayer Prompts

- I praise You Lord that You have drawn me up from …
- Thank You for hearing my cry when …
- You name is holy because You are …
- Thank You for restoring gladness to my life, especially after …

RESPONSE – *Surrender to Him and His ways*

- I confess that my heart is broken over … and I trust You to restore my joy.
- I confess that in my prosperity, I wrongly believed … Help me trust in Your favor alone.
- I have sometimes been dismayed and felt distant because I have …
- Thank You for hearing my plea for mercy.

REQUESTS – *Ask the Spirit to guide your prayer over concerns, resources, and relationships*

- I pray for Your healing grace in the life of … *(name)* as they …
- Lord, even though I am weeping over … give me Your surpassing joy.
- Lord, by Your favor make me strong as I deal with …
- I pray that You will give Your gladness to … *(name)* and sustain them as they …

READINESS – *Encouragement and strength for spiritual battle*

- Do not let the enemy of … have victory over us.
- We cry to You to deliver us from …
- Even when we encounter … we trust You to fill us with joy.

We will sing Your praise and not be silent!

PSALM 31

Commentary by Aaron Telecky
Author   David
Category Lament
In Brief The honest prayer of a man enduring a season of personal trial.

When we bring our troubles to the Lord in prayer, our request is usually for deliverance. Whether through ordinary or miraculous means, our plea is for Him to make our problem go away. But as David's prayer here in Psalm 31 shows, God's plan is often to strengthen our faith by having us walk all the way through the trouble.

To his credit, David begins well, praising God throughout vv. 1-8 for His matchless power and limitless love. Simply put, he knows that God cares for him and that He is more than able to deliver him out of whatever mess he's in. But when he realizes that the Lord's answer wouldn't be immediate relief, he pours out, like a flood, the wildly mixed emotions he had bottled up inside (vv. 9-13).

And once he did that, everything changed. Having experienced a sort of emotional system flush, his heart grew quiet, his head became clear and he recommitted himself to God's care all over again: "But as for me, I trust in You, O Lord, I say, 'You are my God.' My times are in Your hand…" (vv. 14-15a). As a follower of Christ, remember, each of your trials are but one part of a much grander and more glorious plan which is guaranteed to end in eternal victory (v. 19).

So whatever you may be facing today, follow David's lead and take his example to heart: "O love the Lord, all you His godly ones! The Lord preserves the faithful and fully recompenses the proud doer. Be strong and let your heart take courage, all you who hope in the Lord"(vv. 23-24).

Psalm 31 – Guide

REVERENCE – *Identify and celebrate God's praiseworthy attributes*
- God is our refuge and righteous rescuer, our rock and strong fortress – vv. 1, 2, 4, 15, 19
- He leads, guides, and faithfully redeems – vv. 3-5
- He is trustworthy and our source of gladness – vv. 6-7, 14, 21
- Sees and knows our struggles and gives stability/freedom – vv. 7-8
- Hears our admission of rejection, sin, and brokenness – vv. 9-13
- He personally superintends our lives and blesses us – vv. 14-16
- He is abundant in goodness protecting His godly ones from evil – vv. 19-20
- Worthy of our love, He is our faithful source of strength and courage – vv. 23-24

Prayer Prompts
- Thank You that You have led me and guided me to show that Your name is …
- I rejoice that Your love for me has remained steadfast even when …
- Thank You that when I declare "You are my God" I am assured that You are …
- I bless and love You Lord because You have …

RESPONSE – *Surrender to Him and His ways*
- Oh Lord, I commit my Spirit to You as I struggle with …
- Because You see and know me, I surrender my feeling of distress about …
- Because I am a broken vessel, I know I need to trust You for …

REQUESTS – *Ask the Spirit to guide your prayer over concerns, resources, and relationships*
- I pray for … *(name)*, asking You to rescue them from …
- I trust You as my rock and fortress, especially as I deal with …
- Because Your name is … I am trusting You to guide me as I …
- In Your faithfulness, I trust You to preserve … *(name)* as they struggle with …
- You are our hope and blessing, we, as a church, wait on You for …

READINESS – *Encouragement and strength for spiritual battle*
- We trust You to confront the lies of the wicked when they say…
- Hide us from the plots of men when they…

Blessed be the Lord!

PSALM 32

Comments by Jeremiah Porter
Author   David
Category   Lament
In Brief   Without forgiveness we miss out on happiness.

David begins by declaring that people forgiven by God are the happiest, most blessed alive. Their sins are covered; their guilt is removed (v. 1). Those who know the grace of God through Jesus Christ's "once and for all" sacrifice enter a profound rest. This is certainly the experience to which David points in verses 3-5. But this rest begins only when David was willing to trust God enough to confess his sin. Once David confessed his sin he experienced the renewed joy of God's forgiveness.

Psalm 32 intends to call God's people to repentance and confession so they may experience God's deliverance, restoration, and protection (vv. 6-7). In sum, resisting God brings a world of trouble, but trusting God enables His people to abide in His unfailing love (vv. 8-10). Are you confessing your sin before the Lord on a regular basis? Are you afraid of how He will respond to you when you do? Psalm 32 shows us that confession is vital to our spiritual health and, when we do confess, God responds with loving and willing forgiveness.

In praying this Psalm, first praise God (v. 11), for His forgiveness of all your sin. Praise Him for times when you have turned to Him in confession and experienced His presence and forgiveness anew. Second, surrender to God in confession of any current sin. Surrender to His deliverance, protection and unfailing love despite your sin. Finally, request the loving voice of His Holy Spirit's conviction to become louder and louder, and that the lying voice of the evil one, trying to bury us in guilt, is silenced.

Psalm 32 – Guide

REVERENCE – *Identify and celebrate God's praiseworthy attributes*
- He blesses our lives; forgives our transgressions – vv. 1, 2, 5
- Convicts us of our unconfessed sin – vv. 3-4
- Hears our prayers, protects and preserves our lives – vv. 6-7
- Instructs and teaches us personally – v. 8
- Judges the wicked, but surrounds us with goodness and joy – vv. 10-11

Prayer Prompts
- Lord, I am blessed because You have forgiven me for …
- I praise You that You faithfully heard my prayers when …
- Thank You that You were my hiding place and deep joy when …
- Thank You that You instructed my heart and showed me Your way when …

RESPONSE – *Surrender to Him and His ways*
- I confess that sometime my heart can be deceived by …
- I admit my battle with the sin of … often leaves me weak and defeated. Give me grace to confess my sin and experience the joy of Your forgiveness.
- I confess that the temptation of … often causes me to wander from Your will.

REQUESTS – *Ask the Spirit to guide your prayer over concerns, resources, and relationships*
- Give me opportunities to share the gospel of grace and forgiveness with … *(name)*.
- Help me to trust You to be my hiding place right now as I am facing …
- I pray that You will preserve … *(name)* in the midst of their trouble, especially …
- Lord, give Your clear counsel to our church leaders as they are seeking You for …

READINESS – *Encouragement and strength for spiritual battle*
- Let us never forget that wickedness brings sorrow, especially when people …
- We will be glad and rejoice in You, even when …

Your steadfast love surrounds us!

PSALM 33

Comments by Jeremiah Porter
Author   unknown
Category   Praise
In Brief   Fresh encounters with God's sovereign goodness and great-
               ness should result in renewed hope and resounding praise.

The author of this Psalm calls those who are righteous and upright - who have entered into a covenant relationship with God - to sing and shout joyfully to God (vv. 1-3). We are called to sing a new song, which could mean an entirely new song, or perhaps the same song again with a renewed heart of conviction and joy having experienced afresh God's sovereign goodness and greatness. The remainder of the Psalm provides reasons why we ought to praise the Lord.

First, we ought to sing and shout with joy because God's word is right, true, and powerful (vv. 4-9). In verses 6-9 there is a particular emphasis on the power of God's word, evidenced in the creation story when all that God commanded came to be (Gen. 1:1-2:3). The second reason why our hearts should be full of joyful praise is because God is sovereign and His plans and purposes always prevail (vv. 10-11). No person or power can ever thwart God's will. Third, praise ought to flow from our lips because God sees all people, places, and plans on earth (vv. 12-19).

Sometimes we find it easier to put our trust in things we see or experience; sometimes we think it is safer to put our trust in a particular king, kingdom, or resource of power. The truth is, none of these can fully deliver nor protect us from evil and death. God can, however, and His eyes are on those who fear Him and hope in Him (vv. 18-19). For this reason, the writer exclaims, "Blessed is the nation whose God is the Lord" (v. 12).

Concluding with a declaration of dependence upon God (vv. 20-22), the writer notes that the appropriate response to all that is true about God is to wait upon Him with confident expectation. By His timing and in His ways He will deliver on His promises to help us, protect us, and pour out His unfailing love upon us (v. 22).

In praying Psalm 33, we can praise God for ways in which we have seen His word proven true and powerful in our lives. Furthermore, we can wisely surrender once again to trusting God and confessing, if necessary, anything other than Him that may have, inappropriately, received our trust and, therefore, our praise.

PSALM 33 – GUIDE

REVERENCE – *Identify and celebrate God's praiseworthy attributes*
- Inspires songs of joy, thanksgiving, and pursuit of righteousness – vv. 1-3
- He is faithful, righteous, just, and good – vv. 4-5
- He is awesome Creator of all things – vv. 6-9
- Rules over the nations. His plans stand forever – vv. 10-12
- Rules from heaven, all seeing, and all wise – vv. 13-15
- He is faithful and the only hope for salvation – vv. 16-19
- He is holy, our help, our shield, and our source of gladness – vv. 20-22

Prayer Prompts
- We shout to You Lord because … *(various attributes and works)*.
- Thank You that Your upright word teaches me that …
- Thank You that You have always been faithful, especially when …
- I praise You Lord for the assurance that You see and care for me, especially when …

RESPONSE – *Surrender to Him and His ways*
- Lord, realizing You are faithful to me, I confess I have been unfaithful in …
- You love justice, but I admit I have too often been unfair and mistreated … *(name)*.
- Father, I confess that too often I trust… to meet my need, rather than Your steadfast love.

REQUESTS – *Ask the Spirit to guide your prayer over concerns, resources, and relationships*
- Because You are the Creator and Sustainer of the universe, I know I can trust You for …
- Lord, I need Your counsel right now as I …
- Lord, show the plans of Your heart to … *(name)* as they …
- Help me to place my hope in Your steadfast love as I relate to … *(name)*.
- I pray for … *(name)* that You will deliver them from …

READINESS – *Encouragement and strength for spiritual battle*
- Lord, I pray that You will frustrate the plans of … *(ungodly strategies)* as they seek to …
- Lord, I will trust You – and not my own strength, as I face the challenge of …
- Lord, we will wait on You, even when …

We hope in You, our help and shield!

PSALM 34

Comments by Jeremiah Porter

Author   David

Category Praise

In Brief God is worthy to be praised because He cares for us and answers our prayers.

In the first two verses of this Psalm, David establishes his intentions to continually praise God and lift high His name for all to hear, especially those who are suffering, that they might also rejoice (vv. 1-2). David then extends the invitation for all God's people to join in making known the greatness of God (v. 3). Praising is something God's people do both individually and corporately.

David continues by explaining why his heart is so full of praise for God. He tells of his experience in seeking God for help and how God answered his prayers and delivered him from those who wanted him dead (vv. 4-7). He reminds his fellow worshipers that what God has done for him God will also do for all who look to Him (v. 5) and fear Him (v. 7). Thus David invites us all to experience God's goodness by taking refuge in Him (v. 8) and choosing to fear Him. In doing so we will never lack anything we need to do God's will (vv. 9-10). To fear the Lord, David explains, looks like pure and honest speech, repentance, good works, and the pursuit of peace, presumably with God and others (vv. 11-14).

The final section of this Psalm highlights the truth that God sees, hears, responds and cares for His faithful ones (vv. 15-22). He is careful to note that those who belong to God will face trouble and foes (vv. 19, 21), but God hears their cries and responds with deliverance. So, whether a believer is experiencing safety or struggle, he or she has reason to worship because God has delivered His people before, and He will do it again!

As you pray Psalm 34, praise God for ways you have experienced Him answering your cries for help. Praise Him for how such experiences have deepened your trust in Him. Praise Him that He can and will deliver you. As you continue to worship God and wait upon Him, examine your heart and surrender to Him any fear, discouragement or unbelief warring against you. Surrender to His presence as your refuge, strength, and sustenance. Surrender to a deeper fear of Him. Then, ask Him once again (or for the first time) to deliver you from your oppression.

PSALM 34 – GUIDE

REVERENCE – *Identify and celebrate God's praiseworthy attributes*

- He is worthy of blessing, praise, and exaltation – vv. 1-3
- He hears our prayers and delivers us from fear – vv. 4, 6,15,17
- Makes us radiant and free from shame – v. 5
- Rescues the brokenhearted from trouble/affliction; He is good – vv. 6-10, 17-20, 22
- He judges evil – vv. 16, 21-22

Prayer Prompts

- I boast in You Lord because You are …
- I praise You Lord because You have delivered me from …
- Lord, I thank You that I tasted of Your goodness when …

RESPONSE – *Surrender to Him and His ways*

- I confess I have recently spoken evil when I … Cleanse and restore me Lord.
- I confess my temptation to act deceitfully especially when …
- I confess my need to seek and pursue peace in my relationship with … *(name)*. Help me obey You in seeking reconciliation with them today.

REQUESTS – *Ask the Spirit to guide your prayer over concerns, resources, and relationships*

- Because You encamp around me, deliver me from …
- Give me the conviction and power to speak truthfully this week as I …
- Because You are good, I seek You for refuge today from …
- I pray that … *(name)* will sense Your nearness today as they are brokenhearted over …

READINESS – *Encouragement and strength for spiritual battle*

- Lord, today, I will trust You to condemn unrighteousness in the culture, specifically … as I take refuge in You.
- Lord, give me grace to not speak deceitfully, especially when …

PSALM 35

Comments by Dennis Henderson
Author   David
Category Lament
In Brief Great is the Lord; there is none like God. David calls on God
to deal with his enemies rejoicing in what God chooses to do.

Great is the Lord, A Psalm of David is the title of this "imprecatory" lament. In strong terms David asks God to defeat and destroy the enemies of His people.

It is difficult to assign this Psalm to any particular period of David's life. However, the phrasing of verse 1 is similar to what David said to Saul in 1 Samuel 24:15. So it may be linked to the period of David's life when Saul pursued him. In his plea for God's help he anticipates God's deliverance and praises Him as he acknowledges there is none like God (vv. 9-10).

David tells how he has cared for his enemies in the past, yet they have repaid his kindness with evil (vv. 11-16). He questions how long it seems for God to answer him (v. 17). Yet, in the midst of his doubts he thanks God "in the congregation." Corporate praise and thanksgiving always strengthens and compounds the glory God deserves and receives from His people.

He closes the Psalm with praise. How great the Lord is and how God delights in the welfare of his servant (v. 27).

No doubt there are times when we feel like David. Our enemies and troubles surround us. Trust God. He is aware of our situation. In Romans 12:14-21 we are told to do good to our enemies and leave vengeance to the Lord. Grace, praise, and remembering the goodness and sovereignty of God helps us in these times. God will sustain you in the days of betrayal and disappointment.

PSALM 35 – GUIDE

REVERENCE – *Identify and celebrate God's praiseworthy attributes*

- He fights for us – vv. 1-6, 22-26
- Our salvation and joy – vv. 3, 9, 27
- He is our deliverer/rescuer; there is none like Him – vv. 10, 17
- Worthy of thanksgiving and praise – vv. 18, 28
- Our God and Lord, Who sees our affliction and vindicates us – vv. 22-24
- He is Great, righteous, and delights in our welfare – vv. 27-28

Prayer Prompts

- Father, amidst my troubles I shout for joy because You are …
- Father, I will say there is none like You because …
- Lord, I proclaim that You are great because …
- I am grateful that You delight in my welfare and know this is true because …

RESPONSE – *Surrender to Him and His ways*

- Even though You fight for me, I confess I often try to fight in my own strength when I …
- Because You see my troubles, I surrender my… to You and pray "thy will be done."

REQUESTS – *Ask the Spirit to guide your prayer over concerns, resources, and relationships*

- Lord, I trust You to contend for me and vindicate me in my struggle with …
- Because You are great, let me tell of Your righteousness to …
- Because You delight in my welfare, I know I can trust You for …
- I pray for … *(name)* in their battle with … Give them faith to trust You to fight for them.

READINESS – *Encouragement and strength for spiritual battle*

- Because there is none like You, I know You will deliver me from …

Great is the Lord!

PSALM 36

Comments by Dennis Henderson

Author   David

Category   Praise

In Brief   The depravity of a rebellious person who walks far from God compared to the attributes and goodness of the Lord.

The first four verses describe the person who has no fear of God. The words of his mouth are trouble and deceit. He does evil and there is a feeling of hopelessness. He is foolish and exhibits self-deception through his egotism and scheming. Psalm 36 gives us a clear picture of one who rejects the goodness of God and goes his own way.

But Proverbs tell us that the fear of the Lord is the beginning of wisdom (Pr. 1:7). Only God's grace can rescue such a person. That explains why David next turns dramatically to God's attributes (vv. 5-9). God's love is steadfast; He is faithful and righteous.

Acknowledging these wonderful attributes of God calls forth much praise from David. In his understanding the greatness of God and His steadfast love David is alerted to possible exposure to the arrogance of the wicked (v. 11). Praise always makes us aware of our need of dependence on the One who is greater than all. Praise always comes from acknowledging that He is worthy and we are needy.

Daily we are exposed to those who are defiant to God and His kingdom rule in their lives. Reading this Psalm should remind us that greater is He who is in us than all of the influences of Satan's evil ways (1 John 4:4). Let us continue to walk in the truth of the Scriptures, worshiping the One whose steadfast love sustains us daily.

PSALM 36 – GUIDE

REVERENCE – *Identify and celebrate God's praiseworthy attributes*

- Abundant in love and faithfulness; Great in righteousness and justice – vv. 5-6
- He preserves us; He is our refuge – vv. 6-7
- God of abundance and light, He offers us the fountain of life – vv. 8-9
- He loves those who know and delight in Him – v. 10

Prayer Prompts
- O Lord, I worship You today because You are …
- Your unfailing love and faithfulness are like … to my soul.
- You showed me Your great and unfailing love when …

RESPONSE – *Surrender to Him and His ways*

- O Lord, I confess that I have prized … more than Your priceless, unfailing love.
- Because of Your unfailing love, O Lord, I surrender …
- Lord, even though … I will trust that You love me and will preserve me.

REQUESTS – *Ask the Spirit to guide your prayer over concerns, resources, and relationships*

- O Lord, please show Your abundant, unfailing love to … *(name)*.
- Please let … *(name)* know Your faithfulness as he/she deals with…

READINESS – *Encouragement and strength for spiritual battle*

- O Lord, as we engage in spiritual battles today, we look to see how You will display Your … for those who know You and love You.
- May those against You not be able to stop us from glorifying You.

PSALM 37

Comments by Dennis Henderson
Author   David
Category   Wisdom
In Brief   Trust and delight in God in spite of the apparent (and temporary) advantages of the wicked.

Rather than "fretting" because of evildoers, the Psalmist turns our focus to trust, delight, and commitment. Throughout this Psalm David gives direction about what we should be doing. His list is lengthy: "Be still, wait, refrain from anger, turn away from evil, delight, fret not."

With each directive comes a promise and great assurance. The many promises carry wonderful expressions of how God cares for His children. Disaster and famine cannot eternally destroy them (vv. 18-19; cf. Gen. 18:19, Jer. 1:5). On the other hand, the wicked walk on paths of coming destruction (vv. 12-20, 35-36).

David has watched God work through the years and has seen His plans for His children unfold (vv. 25-26). The existence of the empty lives of those who seek their own way is a stark contrast to God's children who are generous (vv. 21-22, 37-40).

Our motivation for generosity comes into full bloom as we see the generosity of God Himself in giving us Jesus. For the eternal God came to earth, becoming poor in the incarnation so that we might become rich (2 Cor. 8:9). This lavish generosity of God in the gospel is supreme motivation for believers today to be radically generous.

This Psalm is eminently practical. It gives us direction for everyday living. In days when nothing appears to be going your way, rest in these verses. No matter the scoreboard of your life right now, rest, wait, trust, and delight yourself in God's character and His Word. He is aware of your situation. And, with David, our perspective is clarified by looking to the eternal and not the temporal.

PSALM 37 – GUIDE

REVERENCE – *Identify and celebrate God's praiseworthy attributes*

- God is our refuge, He protects and provides – vv. 1-4, 22, 24, 40
- He is trustworthy and righteous – vv. 3, 5, 29, 39
- He watches over His people to protect them – vv. 9, 11, 18, 20-23, 28, 32-33
- He delivers from trouble and fear – vv. 33, 39-40
- He is holy and the source of our peace – vv. 17, 37, 40

Prayer Prompts
- Lord, I praise You in the midst of my problems for You are …
- I worship You for being my provider …
- I praise You that You hold an inheritance for me …
- Thank You for being my refuge when …

RESPONSE – *Surrender to Him and His ways*

- I confess I do not trust You when …
- I confess I have weak faith and am becoming weary …
- I confess my anger in wanting to strike back at my enemies …

REQUESTS – *Ask the Spirit to guide your prayer over concerns, resources, and relationships*

- Lord, turn my worry into worship …
  Help me to be patient with …
- Give me grace to seek and pursue peace this week with …
- Teach me to turn to You in my time of need …

READINESS – *Encouragement and strength for spiritual battle*

- Lord, I am trusting You in spite of …
- Lord, Give me grace not to fear …
- Lord, I will trust You and be patient in …

PSALM 38

Comments by Daniel Henderson
Author   David
Category   Lament
In Brief   Clinging to hope in God despite complaining in sorrow.

When we feel great misery over our sin it can seem an unbearable burden. But ultimately it is a blessing because we are compelled to turn to the Lord for restoration and healing. The Lord convicts us of our sin in order to lead us to confession and renewal. The enemy seeks to condemn us for our sin, leading us to unresolved guilt and distance from God. When we fail to understand the destructive consequences of our sin, God will chastise us, as a father does his children (Hebrews 12:5-11) in order to awaken us to the seriousness of our violations and draw us back to abiding fellowship with Him.

Psalm 38 is one of the seven so-called "penitential psalms," (along with 6, 32, 51, 102, 130, 143) and, as such, expresses deep emotion and remorse over sin amid a series of very difficult circumstances. David acknowledges a variety of dimensions of his suffering. He repeatedly admits the burden of severe conviction. While we are not sure of the exact nature and reason for it, David is plagued by painful disease. His sin has brought hardship to his relationships and given his enemies cause for ridicule. This Psalm is not just a picture of heartfelt confession of sin, but an acknowledgement of human injustice and a cry for God's ultimate justice.

David set his heart to wait on God, knowing He would answer (v. 15). With deep sorrow he confessed his sin (v. 18). The Psalm ends with an earnest cry for God to be near, as David's help and only salvation (vv. 21-22).

As we pray from this Psalm, we are reminded of the consequences of sin, our need for immediate acknowledgment and confession. We should always be encouraged in knowing that our Father, through the work of Christ, has given the ultimate sacrifice of love to draw us to Himself and restore our hearts to deep fellowship. He is, indeed, our help and only salvation.

PSALM 38 – GUIDE

REVERENCE – *Identify and celebrate God's praiseworthy attributes*

- He hears/sees us in our desperation and brokenness – vv. 1, 9
- He answers our cry for mercy – v. 15, and never forsakes us – v. 21
- He helps us immediately and saves – v. 22

Prayer Prompts

- Lord, I praise You that You answered me when I needed You to …
- Thank You, Lord, for giving me grace to repent from …
- I praise You for Your saving power that saved me from …
- Thank You for drawing near to me when … opposed my faith.

RESPONSE – *Surrender to Him and His ways*

- I confess that I failed to trust in Your mercy when …
  Demonstrate Your mercy to me, Lord.
- Lord, I need Your powerful grace to set me free from my sin of …
- I confess that I am prone to run from You when I am
  tempted to …

REQUESTS – *Ask the Spirit to guide your prayer over concerns, resources, and relationships*

- Lord, help … *(name)* today as they are walking through a hard season.
- Lord, draw near to me today as I seek to serve You in …
- Give me grace to trust Your timing for …

READINESS – *Encouragement and strength for spiritual battle*

- Lord, I am trusting Your saving power today to help me as
  I battle …
- Lord, help me to trust Your Word today when …
- Lord, rescue … *(name)* from their sin and become their Savior today!

PSALM 39

Comments by Daniel Henderson
Author   David
Category   Confidence
In Brief   Consider the shortness and foolishness of life while waiting on God to answer.

There are seasons in life when our sense of frustration, confusion, and pain stir such deep questions that, if we were to vocalize them to others, it would be spiritually harmful. Yet, God already knows our deepest thoughts and excruciating burdens. Sometimes our perplexity is connected with God's discipline which can be hard to understand to our finite minds. Psalm 39 makes this clear. We are also reminded that, in prayer, we can open our hearts completely to God, admitting a wide array of the real emotions we are experiencing.

Job, trying to make sense of God's hand of testing, expressed emotions similar to David, "I loathe my life; I would not live forever. Leave me alone, for my days are a breath. What is man, that you make so much of him, and that you set your heart on him" (Job 7:16–17). Yet, David offers his similar doubts in the midst of an abiding devotion to God. His complaint is not about God, but *to* God. The longings are ultimately offered in love and loyalty to the Lord, in spite of the bewilderment.

David refused to openly speak of his angst before his enemies, but brought them passionately to the Lord, with a clear understanding of the brevity of his life, and his temporary trials (vv. 4-6). His words seem to parallel the reminder from James, "What is your life? For you are a mist that appears for a little time and then vanishes" (Jam. 4:14). Peter wrote, "though now for a little while, if necessary, you have been grieved by various trials" (1 Pet. 1:6) as he sought to bring proper perspective to Christians facing adversity and persecution.

As the Psalm unfolds, it becomes clear that David's misery is the result of his own sin. He looks to the Lord as his only hope for deliverance, forgiveness, and restoration (vv. 7-13). In the midst of his tears, he desperately needs divine peace and restored joy (vv. 12-13). David returns again to the truth of his fleeting life.

This Psalm is a great reminder that we must come to God with all of our emotions and, of course, the honest acknowledgement of our sin. Life is very brief and none of us wants to squander the opportunities of this short journey by holding on to the sins that destroy our joy, peace, and fellowship with God.

Psalm 39 – Guide

REVERENCE – *Identify and celebrate God's praiseworthy attributes*

- Causes us anguish and works within us to draw us to Him – vv. 1-3, 11
- He knows the number of our days, that our time is brief – vv. 4-5
- He is our hope, saving us from transgression and oppression – vv. 7-8
- He hears our cries/prayer – v. 12

Prayer Prompts

- I praise You that You are eternal because …
- I praise You that You rebuked me when …
- I praise You for Your discipline in my life when …

RESPONSE – *Surrender to Him and His ways*

- Thank You for drawing me back to You …
- I confess that I am silent before You about …
- Help me to remember Your eternal perspective about …

REQUESTS – *Ask the Spirit to guide your prayer over concerns, resources, and relationships*

- Help me to have an eternal perspective in my numbered days …
- God, convict me of my sin of … Gently discipline me so that I …
- God, hear my cry for help about …

READINESS – *Encouragement and strength for spiritual battle*

- God, I know I will rejoice in You again in …
- Lord, help me to look to You for hope in …

PSALM 40

Comments by Daniel Henderson
Author   David
Category Praise
In Brief   Those who seek the Lord during and beyond the dark times of life.

In the opening section (vv. 1-5) David tells how the Lord responded because he had faithfully waited on Him. He encourages readers to "put their trust in the Lord" (v. 3) and describes the manifold blessing of a life of trust (vv. 4-5).

In vv. 6-8 David confirms his commitment to hear and obey God's word. He continues by affirming that he will be faithful to openly declare God's deliverance in his life (vv. 9-10). Yet, as he writes, he is still in the midst of troubles and in need of God's mercy and deliverance. He is still fighting battles with his sin and feels overwhelmed, but rests his faith on the steadfast love and deliverance of the Lord (vv. 11-15).

The Psalm ends with a strong exhortation to seek the Lord and find joy and gladness in Him, regardless of personal failures or lingering trials. We are encouraged to love the Lord and declare his greatness at all times (v. 16). David's humility is notable as he concludes the Psalm with the admission, "I am poor and needy, but the Lord takes thought for me." His final declaration reminds us again that God is our help and deliverer (v. 17).

This Psalm calls us to praise God for answered prayer and past deliverance. We are challenged to live in abiding trust and obedience, as the familiar hymn enjoins, "Trust and obey, for there's no other way to be happy in Jesus but to trust and obey." We should be faithful to gladly declare to others the delivering work of Christ in our lives. But, the trials and failures of this journey will persistently plague us. Whatever may come we must continually seek the Lord, find our joy in Him and always declare, "Great is the Lord!"

He is worthy! We are needy!

PSALM 40 – GUIDE

REVERENCE – *Identify and celebrate God's praiseworthy attributes*

- He hears and responds; He lifts me up; He fills my heart with song – vv. 1-3
- He is wondrous; no one compares to Him – v. 5
- He is faithful, loving, and merciful – v. 10
- He is our help and our Deliverer – v. 17

Prayer Prompts

- I praise you Lord for hearing me and responding when …
- I praise you Lord for setting my feet on a firm place when …
- I praise you Lord for no one compares to You in …
- I praise you Lord for being my help and deliverer by …

RESPONSE – *Surrender to Him and His ways*

- I will wait patiently for You, Lord, in …
- I will declare Your wonders, Lord, to …
- I desire to do Your will, Lord, by …

REQUESTS – *Ask the Spirit to guide your prayer over concerns, resources, and relationships*

- Lord, lift me up out of my pit of … and give me a firm place to stand.
- Lord lift up … *(name);* help them to declare Your wondrous acts.
- Protect me in Your love and mercy Father from …
- I confess my neediness to You Lord; remember me as I …
- I confess my sins of … have blinded me. Forgive me.

READINESS – *Encouragement and strength for spiritual battle*

- By Your mercy, I will declare Your deliverance among …
- I will sing hymns of praise because You have …
- I will wait patiently as You deal with those who are seeking evil against me in …

PSALM 41

Comments by Daniel Henderson
Author   David
Category   Confidence
In Brief   Trusting the Lord for strengthening and healing.

This Psalm can be summarized as an admission of weakness in the midst of attack and betrayal, accompanied by a repeated request for divine grace. David's prayer reminds us of Paul's struggle with his "thorn in the flesh" and our Lord's affirmation to him, "My grace is sufficient for you, for my power is made perfect in weakness" (2 Cor. 12:9).

The Psalm begins with David's description of his present situation. He is poor, weak, in trouble, and even sick. His admission is rooted in his confidence in the protection and preservation of God. From this reality, David cries out two times, "Lord, be gracious to me!" (vv. 4, 10). His needs are personal and interpersonal. Personally, he confesses his sin (v. 4). Interpersonally, he is dealing with severe verbal attacks from his enemies (vv. 5-8) and the pain of betrayal by a close friend (v. 9).

In the midst of this pain, David is assured that God delights in him and will uphold his personal integrity. He is trusting God to defeat his enemies and prays, "set me in your presence forever" (vv. 11-12). This perspective of eternity climaxes the Psalm with David's resolve of praise, "Blessed be the Lord the God of Israel, from everlasting to everlasting! Amen and Amen" (v. 13).

As we apply this Psalm we are compelled to admit our own weaknesses, confess our sin, trust the Lord with the pain of interpersonal attack, and look to him for the victory only He can provide. Our confidence rests in the Lord's promise of abundant grace in and through it all. His grace empowers us to live with endurance and integrity through every battle. And, because of the finished work of Jesus and His salvation in our lives, we can assuredly declare that He will set us in His presence forever. We praise God for eternal life. When these brief trials have ended we will have "no less days to sing God's praise than when we first begun." Amazing grace how sweet the sound, and how constant its provision in all the ups and downs of our earthly trek.

PSALM 41 – GUIDE

REVERENCE – *Identify and celebrate God's praiseworthy attributes*

- God is protector, deliverer, rescuer, and healer – vv. 1-3
- He is gracious defender, preserver, and vindicator – vv. 10-12

Prayer Prompts
- Lord, You are the One who rescues us from …
- Father, You are the healer of …

RESPONSE – *Surrender to Him and His ways*

- Father, today I choose to forgive … *(name)* for … Help me to be grace filled.

REQUESTS – *Ask the Spirit to guide your prayer over concerns, resources, and relationships*

- Lord, since we are to pray for our enemies, today I pray for … *(name)* that they would know Your grace and salvation.

READINESS – *Encouragement and strength for spiritual battle*

- Help me walk in integrity before You today as I …

APPENDIX A

PSALMS BY CATEGORY

Wisdom

Psalms 1, 37

Prophecy

Psalms 2, 16, 22

Lament

Psalms 3–7,10, 12–14, 17, 26, 28, 31–32, 35, 38

Praise/Joy

Psalms 8, 24, 29, 33, 34, 36, 40

Thanksgiving

Psalms 9, 18, 19, 30

Confidence/Trust

Psalms 11, 23, 25, 27, 39, 41

Royal

Psalms 15, 20, 21

APPENDIX B

HISTORICAL CONTEXT AND STRUCTURE OF THE PSALMS

Psalms is a masterfully composed anthology of ancient Israel's songs and prayers that covers almost a millennium of history. Within the 150 chapters, there exists a beautifully complex variety of poetic genres including hymns of joy, lament, thanksgiving, and psalms of confidence, remembrance, wisdom, and kingship. The arrangement of the various themes seems intentionally random, making it difficult on one hand to interpret any given psalm in its original context, but on the other hand making the book of Psalms applicable to a universal audience. Given the broad scope of the composition, it seems best to assume that the historical background of the Psalms is the history of the nation of Israel. This assessment informs and guides the theological implications of the Psalms and, thus, would lead any reader to broadly claim that the theology of the Psalms is the theology of the whole Old Testament.

The early church fathers thought the Psalms were uniquely the microcosm of the Bible. Athanasius (c. 296–373) likens them to the variety within a botanical garden, while Basil the Great (c. 329–79) describes them as a great storehouse. For most of the history of the church they were the layman's major Biblical source of faith and devotion.[2]

The structure of the Psalms is broken down into a collection of five books (which is why *Praying the Psalms* will be released as five separate volumes). While scholars continue to delve into this curious structural component, one leading explanation is that the Psalms are meant to correspond to and reflect the first five books of the Old Testament, also known as the Pentateuch or Torah. In other words, there is an intentional inter-textual relationship between the Torah and Psalms that ought to shape and inform our reading and understanding. Additionally, this relationship seems to remind the original readers that Psalms held equal authority and relevance to the Torah as divinely inspired Scripture. Jewish tradition viewed the Psalms as a second Pentateuch (Torah) and as an echo of the first. So much so that a rabbinic commentary of Psalm 1 states "as Moses gave five books of laws to Israel, so David gave five "books" of Psalms to Israel."[3]

This structural dynamic further comes to light as the beginning Psalm in each of the five "books" seems to transition emphasis and themes that correspond to the Pentateuch. And keeping in step with the overall theme of Psalms, each of the five "books" concludes with a doxology of praise. Consistent with a particular literary device of Hebrew poetry, one scholar relates the five "books" of the Psalms to the Pentateuch in a chiastic, or inverted order.[4] Thus, the Pentateuch ends where the Psalms begin and the Psalms end where the Pentateuch begins. In order to visualize this powerful dynamic, the following chart seeks to summarize the key relational components of the Psalms and Pentateuch:[5]

Pentateuch	Psalms	Theme	Praise
Deuteronomy	Psalms 1-41 (Book 1)	The importance of obedience to God's law.	"Blessed be the LORD, the God of Israel, from everlasting to everlasting! Amen and Amen." ~Psalm 41:13
Numbers	Psalms 42-72 (Book 2)	The trials of God's people and hope for a future restoration.	"Blessed be His glorious Name forever; may the whole earth be filled with His glory! Amen and Amen! ~Psalm 72:19
Leviticus	Psalms 73-89 (Book 3)	The distinct community of God's people marked by faith and holiness.	"Blessed be the LORD forever! Amen and Amen." ~Psalm 89:52
Exodus	Psalms 90-106 (Book 4)	The LORD's liberation of Israel and the wilderness wanderings of the people of God.	"Blessed be the LORD, the God of Israel, from everlasting to everlasting! And let all the people say, "Amen!" Praise the LORD!" ~Psalm 106:48
Genesis	Psalms 107-150 (Book 5)	The LORD's creative and saving intervention in the lives of the faithful.	"Let everything that has breath praise the LORD! Praise the LORD!" ~Psalm 150:6

While the chart above simply provides a concise overview, further study of the Psalms alongside the Pentateuch will promote their striking connection with ever increasing depth and clarity. Yet what is most vital about the relationship between the Psalms and Pentateuch is not how they reference each other, but rather what they both point the reader towards.

It is significant to remember that of all the Old Testament Scriptures that are quoted in the New Testament, Psalms rises to the top of the list just above Isaiah. In their commentary on the Psalms, Bruce Waltke and James Houston note that of the 283 direct quotations of the Old Testament in the New Testament, 116 or 41% of them are from the Psalms.[6] They go on to observe that Jesus alludes to the Psalms over fifty times and then draw the powerful conclusion that "when New Testament writers explicitly cite Psalms, which are written in small letters with reference to David, they write in capital letters with reference to Christ.[7]"

Both the Psalms and Pentateuch, like all of Scripture, ultimately have a cross-worn path and are best interpreted and applied Christologically. A powerful scene of the resurrected Christ in Luke 24 conveys this dynamic with striking clarity when Jesus proclaims to two puzzled disciples, "O foolish ones, and slow of heart to believe all that the prophets have spoken! Was it not necessary that the Christ should suffer these things and enter into His glory?" And beginning with Moses and all the Prophets, He interpreted to them in *all the Scriptures the things concerning Himself* (Luke 24:25-27 *emphasis added*). Just moments later, this "Bible study" with Jesus resulted in the disciple's profound response when they exclaimed, "Did not our hearts burn within us while He talked to us on the road, while He opened to us the Scriptures?" (Luke 24:32). For these two disciples, ignorance was overcome by intimacy as prayer ("He talked to us on the road") and the word ("He opened to us the Scriptures") converged and empowered them to testify to what God had done (cf. Acts 6:4). Jesus reiterates this vital truth of all Scripture being fulfilled in Himself one more time before He commissions all of His disciples to proclaim the gospel, "Then He said to them, 'These are My words that I spoke to you while I was still with you, that everything written about Me in the Law of Moses and the Prophets and the Psalms must be fulfilled'" (Luke 24:44). All of the correlating themes of the Pentateuch and Psalms, then, are fulfilled in the person and work of Christ, which elicits a heartfelt response of praise.

As one writer put it, "If the Bible's narrative materials relate what God has done and the prophetic literature reports what God has said, the Psalms present the response of the people to the acts and words of God."[8] So as we journey through *Praying the Psalms,* may we, with burning hearts, respond in the same way David did in Psalm 40:5 when he declared, "You have multiplied, O LORD, my God, your wondrous deeds and your thoughts toward us; none can compare with you! I will proclaim and tell of them, yet they are more than can be told."

End Notes:

2. Waltke, B. K., Houston, J. M., & Moore, E. (2010). *The Psalms as Christian Worship: A Historical Commentary* (p. 117). Grand Rapids, MI; Cambridge, U.K.: William B. Eerdmans Publishing Company.

3. William G. Braude, *The Midrash on the Psalms* (New Haven: Yale University Press, 1959), vol. 1, p. 5.

4. Vassar, S. John. *Recalling a Story Once Told: An Intertextual Reading of the Psalter and Pentateuch.* Mercer University Press, Macon, GA, 2007, p.9-10.

5. The themes section of the chart are influenced and summarized from: Vassar, S. John. *Recalling a Story Once Told*

6. Waltke, B. K., Houston, J. M., & Moore, E. (2010). *The Psalms as Christian Worship: A Historical Commentary* (p. 110). Grand Rapids, MI; Cambridge, U.K.: William B. Eerdmans Publishing Company.

7. Ibid.

8. Limburg, J. (1992). Psalms, Book of. In D. N. Freedman (Ed.), *The Anchor Yale Bible Dictionary* (Vol. 5, p. 522). New York: Doubleday.

 STRATEGIC RENEWAL

Our greatest need is Jesus Christ living through a revived church.

Strategic Renewal's vision is to see praying Christians supporting praying pastors who lead praying churches into supernatural gospel impact. Every revival in history that resulted in a spiritual awakening in society always began in movements of extraordinary prayer.

Strategic Renewal is igniting the heart of the church through practical resources, extraordinary events, and equipping pastors for a renewed emphasis on Scripture-Fed, Spirit-Led, Worship-Based Prayer.

THE 6:4 FELLOWSHIP

Pastors Committed to Prayer and the Ministry of the Word

The 6:4 Fellowship, a ministry of Strategic Renewal, exists to facilitate a Christ-exalting reawakening of pastors to the sufficiency of *prayer and the ministry of the Word of God* as their leadership priorities.

The priorities declared in Acts 6:4 define New Testament leadership. These clear, God-ordained priorities gave early church leaders the courage to say "no" to the distractions of lesser demands in order to focus on the core of supernatural ministry.

The 6:4 Fellowship is a diverse, international pastor-to-pastor community. It is not oriented around a single ministry or personality. It is cross-denominational in make-up and led by a team of pastors who exemplify the values of Acts 6:4 and is focused as much on what pastors are becoming as on what they are doing.

The Fellowship unites hearts around a vision for a church committed to prayer and the ministry of the Word and through the power of God's Spirit. When Christ is honored and His mission for this world is pursued His way, things will change.

Join the movement today! Learn more about our pastoral community and sign up for free weekly resources at
www.64fellowship.com